Relevancy of YOGA IN LIFE

by

Acharya Shakti Nath Pandey

Winsome Books India

ISBN : 81-88043-65-6

First Published 2010

Published by :

Winsome Books India

209, F-17, Harsha Complex, Subhash Chowk,
Laxmi Nagar, Delhi - 110 092
Ph. : 011-65845445
E-mail : winsomebooks@rediffmail.com
admin@winsomebooks.com
Website : www.winsomebooks.com

The Book is Dedicated on lotus feet of

Shri Pavan Putra Hanumanji

And

to my father Late Shri Amarnath Pandey

a Great Warrior of Four Indian Wars

and also a Warrior of life.

The Fear of life, The Storms of life
The Thunders of life, The Quakes of life
The Waves of life, The Currents of life
The Burdens of life, The Flows of life
The Struggles of life, The Conflicts of life
The Devils of life The Fears of life,
The Uncertainties of life, The Insecurities of life,
The Speeds of life, The Problems of life

And the changes of life are not less than the fears of death, Passing through the terrible eras of life and happenings of life have lost peace, patience, certainty with pleasures. No one is pleased, no one is satisfied. Where all these have been gone? Do you need all such necessities of human lives? Then just go through this book and go through Yoga. Yoga is the only life philosphy which gives ever – the life & life & life. Since the agoes. Yoga is doing such. There is no need to ask authenticity of Yoga. It has been certifying it self since last many agoes. Just walk on the way of Yoga and live life....... live life......... live life.........

- **Acharya Shakti Nath Pandey**

BIBLIOGRAPHY

1. Patanjali Yog Darshan **2.** Patanjali Yog Pradeep **3.** Hath Yog Pradeepika **4.** Shree Mad Bhaagvadgeeta **5.** Yog Vaasistha **6.** Naarad Puran **7.** Manu Smriti **8.** Vivek Chudamadi **9.** Shiv Maha Puran **10.** Shri Mad Devi Bhagavat Maha Puran **11.** Panch Dashi **12.** Naradeeya Bhaktisutra **13.** Yog Meemaansaa **14.** Ashtaavakra Geeta **15.** Sri Ram Charit Maanas.

VOCABULLARY

Anubhuti - Realization, Astaang - Eight Parts, Asteya - No Thefting
Aparigraha - No collection, Ahinsa - Non violence,
Brahmcharaya - No Sex, Baahya - Outer, Antah - Inner
Dhaarnaa - Keeping Ability, Eashwar - Almighty (God)
Sthir - Stable, Siddhi - A Devine Power in Person
Samadhi - To reach in stage of Zero / God, Nirodh - To Stop
Shauch - Cleanness/Piousness, Santosh - Satisfaction
Kaivalya - Nothing else except the God, Tatva - Element
Anant - Limitless, Eashwar Pranidhan - Devotion on God

To him ....

Acharaya Shakti Nath Pandey has a very genious personality in him and he has studied several life problems of today's people.

This book **Relevancy of Yoga in life** deeply says the psychological analysis of individuals of present era. Not only this but it also analyses, admires, inspires, the people to make the life positive by thoughts, by sentiments, and by good behaviours.

Many-many Yoga books are in market today and they all have worked hard for a good book of yoga. But this book really shows the way of Yoga.

I hope that after reading this book every one will feel deeply that Yoga may give a real life. I have been never a person inerested in Yoga, whether I have studied several kind of books Subjects continuously till my all over life. I was born in that family where scholarship was a common usual behaviour of my family & relatives. Fortunately a day came to me by Acharya Shakti Nath's effords and I studied the book, really its so deep study of human nature & human life. hope all well wishes to him and to this book.

Deepawali
2009,
Kashi

Associate Professor
Dr. Rajneesh Shukla
Head of Department
Deptt. of Comparative Religions Study
&
Noddle Officer
University Grant Commission
for Dr. Sampurnanad Sanskrit University,
Varanasi.

About the Author

Author of this bo›k Acharya Shakti Nath Pandey was born on 13.03.1971 his father was a military personnal. His belonging is with a reputed Kanyakubja Brahmin family.

After Eighth Class he became a student of Sanskrit in a college of Dr. Sampurnanad Sanskrit University, Varanasi. At the same time he joined Maharshi Mahesh Yogi's Ved Vigyan Vidyapetham and he studied Sanskrit, Vedas, Puranas well as with various kind of Yogas. Many other Indian desciplines of knowledge he learn't their as Jyotish, Palmestry, Ratna, Yoga, etc. He learnt such several knowledges in Mahesh Yogi's Educational Institutions at various places from Delhi to South India upto six years. Laterly, he became a Mukhya Acharya in the same group and as a special teacher of Yagya, Yoga, Jyotish & Yoga he worked there in these Institutions from Noida (U.P.), Bhitaura (Fatehpur, U.P.) Sihora (M.P.) to Budani, Best Godwari (A.P.) upto 4 years. Mean while he completed his Shastri Degree (Graduation in Sanskrit) from Dr. Sampoornanand Sanskrit Univeristy and completed his B.A. from Allahabad University.

After that he joined G.T.S. College Bombay and completed Acharya degree in Sanskrit as well as M.A. from Univerisιy of Allahabad.

In Mumbai he worked as a Yoga, Veda, Karmakand and Yagya teacher. He tought Karmakand and Practical Acharyatra to several people. From his own place, several kind of Yoga he tought there upto years.

Excluding all such the Author worked in several Kathaa (Sri Mad Bhagwat Katha) & Yagya programmes as Mukhya Aacharya till the years.

He studied and analysed the Yoga's relevancy for today's life and did the book.

Publisher

Pearl - House

Four Words

Since the many years from my very innocent childhood days I was in studies of Sanskrit, Vedas & Yoga. I started my life from a very renouned instituions of Yug Purush (The Era Person) Maharshi Mahesh Yogi's Sanskrit and Yogpeeth (University) Ved Vigyan Vidyapeeth.

I am still in the way of Yoga life in Mumbai, whether, its a big Metropolitan city where people are struggling day & night for life.

I ever feel their problems which are often psychological & Ideological. They have dipped deeply in them. I feel pain for them. I thought till the years that they may solve, more than eighty percent of their problems by Yoga. But now I may say to them please listen me. One day God inspired me the way to say them and that was an idea writting a book for these working people.

I know that book is not so deep but it is really intreresting what they need. They need a guideline in light way in easy words. Book analyses several aspects of common individuals who are known and called - 'Crowd'. This will show a new life way to them. I have tried to touch various aspects of life and Yoga whether the language of this book is not a language of a very typical Yoga scholar because it is for common individuals. So it is in common language. Even many of the English words are common and adopted in Yoga literature have not been used so that every one may understand the Yoga without any technicality of yoga with thanks to God. Om Swasti.

— Acharya Shakti Nath Pandey

PEARL

THE OPENING

Many many kinds of human races are dwelling on the earth Since the past, this kind of variety of human races was available. Even as various races of humans have been in past and are present. In the same way their places, life styles, works, foods, climates & cultures are different. But one thing is common in them sentiments, success & failure's effects, realizations and need of peace.

Indian life on earth is the ancient one in all of these races. Indian Rishis, Saints & several other Scholars, Researches of life & life problems worked till thousands of years and they found the problems of human life are not bothering nor disturbing as because of their beingness in outer world but these are real problems for humans because these are heavily effecting to the inner world of human bodies. Thus they started to search the methods & way of balancing & keeping natural stages well of human bodies. So that they can face and win over the outer world's problems.

By the Researches of several Scholars, Researchers, Saints & Rishis many many ways of life processing well and best as it was before the problems they searched. All these ways of life managing got a name of Yoga. Various kinds of Yogas are present now life Bhakti Yoga, Prem Yoga (Love Yoga with God), Karm Yoga, Sankhya Yoga, Sanyas Yoga etc. By Yoga's way in any kind of problems and in every kind of life situations an individual may pass as easily like an innocent child's play and no more harms he will get in his mind, body, psychology nor in his elemental bodies.

Yoga is the way of life management in which an Individual may recharge his self by his self just by a few practices. But Yoga is a complete life philosphy in which basic practices of some life Principles are needed to be practiced by an individual upto its highest point neither the rather practices of Yoga like Pranayam and Dhyaan will not give excellent results. So whenever one goes from Yoga way he needs the principle parts practices peacefully with deep patience, so that he may store a real energy of Supernatural world. Yes there are three worlds one is outer world means worldly world of materials & lives, another world is self world means an individuals inner world in which all kind of keys of relationship rooms of Supernatural powers are kept and the third world is the unseen world in which all kind of Super natural powers are existing.

Thus the basics of Yogas Philosophy are dependents of this theme. Present worlds mentalities of such words 'I don't believe' are not implacable nor admittible in any kind of Yoga's way. The Yoga starts from the way of believes, ends on faith with achievements of all Kind of Natural, Worldly, Spiritual, Materialistic, Personal, Social Natural and Supernatural successes. At a time one can work with Yoga life & worldly life this is another magic of Yoga. In fact Yoga is not a magic but it may say and pays magic results to its practioner. The trainees of Yoga feel that they are being better than their Previous & Past life. They feel real, Pious, worthful and pleased. This is not merely an imagination but in fact it becomes a biological, psychological, elemental, ideological & behaviourial stage of their lives.

Yes, this is the Yoga which changes all kind of changes in life at a time really its not less than a magic. An individual may get changes in health (Biological changes) as well as with before said fields of life like ideology, psychology etc. Thus an individual in fact needs a real knowingness of Yoga and its detail Philosophies. It means an individual must have to be a very good reader of Yoga. Then throughly he must understand the subject with help of a Yoga Master and then he should start the Yoga practices.

Here in this book, seeing the real problems of today's life and problems of individuals of world class people the tries of narrations of all life problems and yoga have been maintained. Another good thing of this book is in view of writer was kept continuously that an unknown person of Yoga, Yoga philosophy may understand Yoga basically. So that he may start the practices of life principles like Truth, Non-violence etc. And by that he may enable his soul, his body, his confidence within a short period.

Latterly Yoga is a very typical way of life if the basic practices of life principles are not completed no one can get the climax result points of Yoga. So here in this book the basic learning opportunities by the reader of any class, age, and any geographical region has been contributed successfully, with this view book is magically successful and the practitioner may reach by his self upto the climax.

As per need a new practioner of Yoga may repeat and may make perfect his practices of life principles thus also he will reach upto the highest results of Yoga. Whether this is not a guarantee letter but this is a real status of book theocratically. And as per need a practioner should take a help of real Yoga Teacher who has gotten certain results of Yoga field. Yoga pays a lot of success in every field so one should must inquire the Teacher that what kind of success he has achieved. ❑

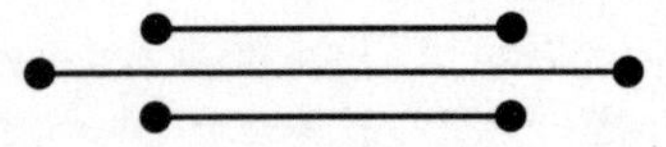

PEARL

LIFE IN PAST, PRESENT & FUTURE

What an individual is living today that all is a total result of his past and what Something he will live in future that will be the total achievment of present. There, in such life living process a lot of mental, ideological, sentimental, expected or unexpected achievements, problems, short commings, failures & successes come which are often not presumed nor imagined or analysed to come in his life. Due to all such unexpected results of life a person becomes bothered. Sometimes these are normally faced by some one because these are normal but sometimes these are out of range of a persons capability thus he becomes tensed and stressed.

Such stresses create many problems for his life, for his stemna, sentiments, couerage, peace and to living wills also. If these stressess continue upto a long period these become the causes of damages of personality and a lot of sicknesses in ideological, psychological, minute & elemental personalties start to come.

This kind of sicknesses, naturally effect the biological, chemical and geographical bodies. These are the causes due to which we see many persons suddenly changed heavily by their biological & geographical bodies within a short period. Some one was shocked due to the decieves of his friends, family, relatives, masters, workers, husband, wife, servants, helpers, partners or children, because results were just opposite as he was expected. A particular person on whome he was having faith as his best nearest person but his approach resulted just against to his expectations the believer becomes unable to bear all that. His mental harms, loosing of patience and courage started and he failed in life. His chemistry & biology disturbed due to the psychological disorders.

In the same same way losses of buisness or other kind of big or many short problems may harm to same one heavily. By that he may be badly damaged. Such studies of life must be known by a Yoga practioner so that he may remove his problems by his self in the way of Yoga. Just to study some one's life shortly we can see it in three parts Present, Past and Future.

A. Life in Past

- **(a) Personal life**
- **(b) Family life**
- **(c) Social life**
- **(d) Financial life**
- **(e) Total achievements**
- **(f) Disorders**
- **(g) Substances.**

Here in this part, we are discussing the past effects in some one's personality by his past life. Because every life in present or in future is basically a dependent of past. Thus the basics of past life are often continued in present life and then after to the future life. So whenever going to solve the psychological problems of a person, its a need that what was his past. Thus every one must be a good analyser of his self and by Yoga it may be solved.

(a) Personal Life : Some one's personal life either he is a child or an old person creates several things in his personality. Either he feels well or weak, Negative or positive. If some one has enough time & chance to live his life satisfactorily he might be getting an enough healthy personality of psychological factors. And thus his past may create a good present. But if he was unpleased with his personal life then he may be sick in present.

(b) Family Life : Every one is born as a unit of a family and till the life and also before and after the life this attachment goes continue. This is an Indian study. In other many continents & religions also such kind of short studies are present. This is not a believe only. Thus every one is ever related psychologically with his family. Whether where short families have been a fashion, there people are suffering from a lack of psychological & sentimental satisfaction of family.

(c) Social Life : This sentimental satisfaction of family gives pleasures, peace and patience inside the body. But in lack of that or by nature a few persons search it in society. Social life's satisfactions and dissatifactions also effect to some one.

(d) Financial Life : In today's life financial stages of a person are most important which are often unavoidable. As the satisfactions & dissatisfactions from family & society are important in the same way the financial satisfactions are also important. Totaly a personality depends on these factors that in past what kind of stages were past in some one's life. That causes the basics of his present life.

(e) Total Achievments : As the life is pleasant with psychological normalities from family and society as well as with financially good stages. The achievements of a person in past life also pay him a good or bad present personality and life. Total achievements means all kind of life achievements of a person either these were in personal life or in social or family life, financial or other kind of all these cause very much for present.

(f) Disorders : If the needed & expected sentimental satisfaction from family were not gotten or socially also some one was dissatisfied or avoided, financial stages were also not well then a person depends to save his self on his achievements but if these were also not well then naturally it creates certain sickness light or deep.

(g) Substances : Because the world is crowded to much now and no one can live satisfied with his life so it is obvious to go in psychological stress and that may cause other problems - Yoga normalize the past and removes the past effects. It normalizes the all bodies as according to the present.

B. Life in Present

(a) Personal life **(b) Family life** **(c) Social life**
(d) Financial life **(e) Total Achievments**
(f) Disorders **(g) Substance**

One's present life whether depends basically on past but it may be changed and built well on new pattern. But for a new era of life every one needs many things in support. For future he must plan and should work wisely so that his life may be well in present & in future. Even then many kind of anxieties may be living in one's life. So its a need to analyse all parts and then should plan.

(a) Personal Life : Many times due to lack of means & supports an individual lives not well in his personal life. He goes in several kind of unnecessary thoughts. But if the family life, social life and financial stages are well an individual can live peacefully. And no kind of insecurity feeling may take place in his mind. Thus it is a need of someone that to live well. He must be satisfied with his life.

(b) Family Life : What was the past family life and its support or satisfactions from family may be recovered if the present stages and environment of family is satisfactory and good. So every one needs (Whether many do not feel like that) to collect his family and should try to make please them. It's a natural duty too. It enables to anyone if he is a part of a combined family. Family is a power.

(c) Social Life : Social recognitions and social status is a good thing for every one. If family stages are well every one can live well in society. Social cooperations social supports enable to some one's personality. A few persons' social area or field may be very short or very vidor. It goes person to person differently.

(d) Financial Life : Many kind of depressions, failures, shocks are removed if financial life of a person is running smothly. Thus every one tries to earn much more and enough for his life. This financial life also effects deeply to a personality in all kind of bodies.

(e) Total achievements : Total achievements of someone's life are total cause of personality's is health mental, psychological, biological and others. Many kind of tension, shock effects, depressions, anxieties & other stresses may be removed automatically in a natural process of biological functions if the achievements are satisfactory. But if these are not enough a person may live in stressess.

(f) Disorders : Just to fulfill ambitions and targets every one works hard, in another part of life he faces several psychological problems financial managements of his own life and works. In all such fields a person works alone by his self and some where he gets tensions & certain disorders certainly.

(g) Substances : When disorders are in present life it is a certain stage that in future too these will continue. So it's a need to manage all these well in present so that the future may be saved and successes of future may be kept safe. By Yoga Present and Past both lives of a person are curable. But know the real way of Yoga there is a need of Yoga studies too.

C. Life in Future :

(a) Plannings & Capabilites	**(b) Achievements & Failures**
(c) Changes of Circumstances	**(d) Personal Life**
(e) Financial Stages	**(f) Total Achievements**
(g) Family life	**(h) Social life**
(i) Disorders	**(j) Substances.**

One's past life represent and give platform for present life and present creates chances for future. Often it has been seen that if some one is failed in past his present is well and if present is failed future may be well but a few persons are also there whose all lives are not well. Naturally it causes deep stressess.

(a) Plannings & Capabilities : Every one designs his life for future as according to his brain power but often many false calculations are also made. But a few free style individuals manage all kind of future plans. Free stylers also make false & wrong plans. But these are needed for all as according to their capabilities. When some one analyses his future as in comparision of his ambitions many times he feels very depressed because every one can not achieve his ambitions, so fastly. Then they feel failed, anxious and hopeless.

(b) Achievements & Failures : It's an obvious process of life that when an individual will go to live his life many kind of achievements and failures will come. There is a lot of percentage of such people who become very nervous due to the failures. They couldn't manage normally to their selves infront of the failures. Whether they encourage them too much by the achievements. So they become tensed and stressed this may change their selves.

(c) Chages of Circumstances : Many kind of expected circumstances and changes of assessed future may change till when a person reaches to face these as according to his future's plannings. By that no one should feel nervous but should amend his own plannings. Many times the well running process of plans changes suddenly due to some happenings and then also a typical stage comes.

(d) Personal life : Due to several kind of pressures, burdens, stresses, liabilities, duties, targets lac of means or other problems an individual's personal life goes in tight corners and expected or needed structure or habitual process of personal life becomes disturbed it may create much more tensions.

(e) Financial stages : If as according to the plannings earnings and expenses are well and needed savings are also being good as according to the further planings till then a person feels normal. But if there is a big gap in planned expectations of earnings, expenses and savings then naturally individual goes in anxiousness. If these are not managed shortly normal then the long tensions of such problems may cause psychological problems.

(f) Total achievements : If someone fails in one field or some one's life's one factor is failed then too he might be achieving well success in another field. And calculatively if he is achieving average achievements for his life & he may live normal but if the achievements are not even in average stage toc, he may go inside the many kinds of tensions & hope lessness.

(g) Family Life : If success and failures are well supported by one's family then a person feels encouraged and may live normal and well. But if some one has some family stresses too or lack of family either its support is nill then a person feels alone in world against the life challenges & problems.

(h) Social Life : There is a total lack of all kind of healthy supports in social life today, so no one can feel as well in social circles for his personal problems. Thus a lot of tensions he often needs to face alone.

(i) Disorders : Here a very few aspects of individual's life has been briefly talked so that persons may think on such problems also. Because there are a lot of problems due to which individuals are being abnormally tensed.

(j) Substance : Just to maintain normal and well in such burdens and struggles of life and to leave the abnormality came in life Yoga is the best way. Yes, Yoga helps within short periods, than several medicines and other therapies Yoga is the best one. ❑

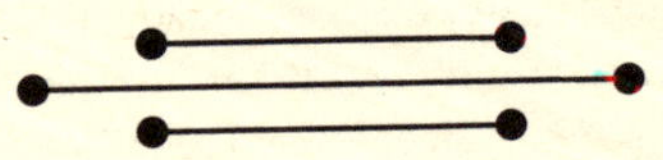

HUMAN BODY AND ITS COMPONENTS

(a) Geographical Body (b) Minute Body (c) Chemical Body
(d) Biological Body (e) Elemental Body (f) Ideological Body
(g) Religious Body (h) Spiritual Body (i) Behavioral Body
(j) Imaginative Body (k) Psychological Body.

In fact in a human body there are a lot of components which are visible and invisible boath. Boath kind of components create a complete structure of human body. Whether these are known or not known by a person but they work as by their natural nature. If any component becomes ill, less, week, increased or decreased abnormality starts in a body. So its a need to know shortly to all these compents, so that an individual may live aware of all kind of changes in body.

There are a lot of systems and components of body but here some main factors are being shortly discussed. A human body has several bodies inside it and these are - **(a)** Geographical body **(b)** Minute Body **(c)** Chemical Body **(d)** Biological Body **(e)** Elemental Body **(f)** Ideological Body **(g)** Religious Body **(h)** Spiritual Body **(i)** Behavioural body **(j)** Imaginative body **(k)** Psychological body.

All these bodies and their several components are inside this one human body. All these are dependents and supporters of each other by the natural system. That system of every body is slightly different to another body. There are rarely a few two bodies which have most of the accurately same systems in twins only. But these twin bodies also have some differences like one will be main and another will be supportive body. But excluding the twins every other body has enough differences of natural nature of their bodies.

A. Geographical Body :

The geography of body means the structure of body may be said biological body but the bearing power of geographical & envlornmental natural pressures are a different virtue & potency of a body so this is called geographical body. This geographical body gets changes due to the change of geographical changes, environmental changes, chemistry of body, ideology and psychology of body.

These geographical changes are often more clear when a child is developing or a young chap (14-15 yrs. boy) is being matured either a 30 yrs youngman is being adult or a 45 to 48 yrs. person goes towards old age symptoms and lastly when an old person of 70 yrs. become more old. When his neck bents down, his face gets a lot of changes eyes, teeth leave his companionship. But such kind of geographical changes' speed may break its process may change in slow speed and the geography of body may be kept till long period by the Yoga exercises.

B. Minute Bodies :

This Biological, geographical body may not be carried by itself. It may not work by it self it needs a life energy which is kept in a fort of minute bodies. This Minute Bodies Fort is invisible but by Yogis it may be seen and may be enterupted or changed too.

These minute bodies are also in three layers **(i)** Sooxma Shareer = Minute Bodies **(ii)** Bhaav Shareer = Feelings Bodies **(iii)** Kaaran Shareer = Cause Bodies.

These are also having many number of these invisible minute bodies as (i) Sooxma Shareer = Minute Bodies have a number of 52 bodies inside their layer. Secondly (ii) Bhaav Shareer (Feelings Bodies) have 28 minute, invisible and very sensitive bodies inside their layer of minute bodies. Thirdly (iii) Kaaran Shareer (Cause Bodies) also have a number of 28 minute strong and causing bodies inside their layer. All these 108 minute bodies keep the soul well saved inside it. And without the Biological Bodies or other bodies only minute bodies keep the soul inside its Fort before the Birth and after the death. Only all these minute bodies are capable to activate the body. When these minute bodies go out of the body soul goes with these and body becomes dead.

C. Chemcial Body :

Inside this Biological Body every one has a chemical body too. It starts from skin and ends inside the bones' enterior region. At every movement the natural chemistry works inside the body. Every veins, tissues, cells, bones, joints and several other big organs and parts of body are working as a chemistry system. Either the disation of food, is being worked by body or the digested past of food being redigested and being convereted in blood and enzymes or in other forms needed in body, is a chemical system of the body.

When a person is normal his all over chemistry is well but when he has taken unwanted materials in his food or he come in deep stresses and mental tensions his all energy which is a working component of body's chemical system goes to solve the tensions, stresses and problems. When chemical system's energy's use starts in stresses and it continues till long period the chemistry of body looses and the results comes on the screen of face and body's outer parts. Body starts loosing energy and naturalness of body. It becomes week.

Thus several kind of physical and mental deseases start in body and life of individual becomes unpleasant. Without diseases also may some one weak and unpleased.

There is no way except the medicines to recover the chemical problems. But Indian Scholars searched a way to systamize the chemistry of body without any medicine and that way is known as Yoga. Yoga needs nothing except the practices of its exercises.

D. Biological Body :

If the study of body starts first of all the Biological shape of any body comes in mind and in eyes also. But when the study is forwarded to later studies scholars get that Biological body alone is not all thing in a body. It is just a component of the body but this is the main & basic component of body. This body is the base and house for all bodies and other components to dwell in it.

Biological Body keeps minute bodies, geographical shapes of body chemical bodies (Chemical System), elemental, Psychological and other bodies in it. All these components of the body, enable each other, support to each other save to each other in growth, in existence, in works, in all natural-unnatural works and processes of the body. But some times due to more work or load on one body the other bodies become effected or sick. Due to this abnormality or breaking of natural process in one body all bodies creates a new change in them. That change may or may not be visible but that becomes negative.

If the breaking of natural process in body is big, deepar till long duration the change also may be big deep or hellious. But if the breaking is not big deep or lengthy in period it may be lightly effecting on body.

But there is one thing very genuine and serious to know that if any kind of body is passing through abnormality certainly all the bodies will become effected. By food, by hard works by hungers, by less rests, by short & light sleeps, by tensions, by deep and lengthy stresses of veins and body all kinds of bodies get changes. And this has been proved that by such effects often the changes are negative. May thse negative changes harmfull manageable by the body, non manageable lightly or deeply harmfull for the body. So care for all kind of bodies is must for a body holder.

Every biological body is also a component of uncountable minerals, enzymes, veins, tissues, cells, bones, hairs and other little and big organs. This body becomes effected also by heat, water, weather, air, cold, summer-winter, thurst, hunger, sleeps, sentiments, tensions, stresses, hard work, no work, grieves, dipressions, pleasures and other uncountable effective factors of body are present on the earth. So the proper knowingness of own body and the effective factors every one should know and should keep in mind ever.

Another most important factor of body is meal/ food. What kind of foods some one takes and what kind of foods are needed to his body, these are two things. Every body has a different ratio of several minerals, chemical items, juices, liquids, waters, vitamins and others. But often it has been seen that persons do not know that what they eat and what their body needs.

For example one body has ironic structure of it and it needs more ironic items in food but the owner of body is not knowing even then the subconsious brain will inspire to the body owner to eat those items in which iron is oftenly much more than other foods. This unknown knowingness of body exists as special energy of body in it. But if the naturality and natural functions of body will becomes disturbed naturally this energy will be used in normalizing the body and the superness of body will get lost.

In modern life from food to works, every kind of bodies are continuously passing from tranision stages by that the stemina and potencies of bodies are decreasing so fastly that's why the geographical bodies of the humans are fastly changing their shapes.

Neither, since before 20 to 30 years people were not loosing the geographical shapes of bodies upto their old age and they were more well and pleased with few means than today.

E. Elemental Body :

The Universe is made by five elements water, earth, fire, air and sky/space. Every thing of the universe is made by all these five elements as with a different ratio. In the same way human bodies are also made by these five elements and the ratio in every body is shortly different. In some bodies fire element is in a big ratio due to that they feel more hunger, much anger and more laziness. In some bodies water is in much ratio they are so enjoying, helping, pleased and soft nature individuals. In this kind of study we get that every element which is prominent in a body it dominates to other elements and due to that the nature of persons are different to each other.

These elemental bodies of humans are also existing inside the biological body of the humans. Due to the different ratio of elements the geography, colours and nature as well as with psychological and ideological behavior also changes in each one. And this may be chan- ged by changing the ratio of elements. Yes the elemental changes are possible by changing the food and the supplies of different elements to the body are possible by effords. One can change his chemistry, psylogical nature, ideological and behavioral nature so fastly with a biological change but the geographical change in body goes with a minimum speed than other bodies change speed. This is also a part of yoga.

How many verieties of body (Human Body) are existing in the world all these are different due to elemental setup either these differences are geographical, biological or psychological as well as chemical & behavioral. The elemental bodies are directly being governed by minute bodies in Biological body. Elemental bodies are creating the causes of chemistry because the elemental bodies are not only dependents of food, many elements are coming from nature, as for air, space (sky) and light is being received from nature directly. As these elemental bodies are receiving such elements these are being enheal then or weak strong or soft. These five elements are lords of different organs in body. As – fire is lord of eyes, Air is lord of skin, water is lord of tongue, earth is lord of nose and space is lord of ears.

Imbalance of earth element effects the breathing and smelling, Imbalance of Air effects the touch and skin, imbalance of water creates the problems of tongue and taste, and imbalance of fire (lights) creates the problems of eyes, and the space imbalance in body creates the problems of ears and hearings. This is a very ancient and basic research of body in India. Yoga is basically based on these elemental facts.

If one element of body is in stage of imbalance from its natural stage in a particular body, then the all four elements go in stage of imabalance. And by that all the bodies get imbalances in them in the same ratio. Till when imbalances are light & minute the effects on biological and in other bodies are also light and minute. But when these are deep and heavy the changes & effects on all bodies as well as with biological seem badly. Such heavy imbalances are causes of sickness. Changes of elemental ratio cause the change of nature in body. Actually every-body (Every individuals' body) has a particular natural nature and these elements are the big balancers & deciders of such natural nature of any body. But such natural natures are also changeable upto a certain limit, but sometimes only such kind of practiced achievements of changes in natural nature may go till any limit.

This elemental setup in body causes the weatheric bearance, and of weatheric stages in environment to keep well the particular body as how it may live well. Actually this is a natural stage of body as according to whose nature, a particular person of a particular human body feels such natural weatheric stages negative or positive for him.

Yoga has a magical power to change to balance the imbalances without any artificial means. Hardly it takes the help of human body and the help of all five elements. By the practices of Yoga again the elemental setup easily comes to its natural stage. Not only this but the potency and stemna may be improved and the elemental system may become more powerful than before.

F. Ideological Body:

In fact Ideological body is basically dependent of memories, as on the platform of memories the ideological body of a person is nitted with elemental and minute bodies.

Yes there is a big importance of minute bodies too elemental and minute bodies of a human body are working as with the help of an individuals ideological bodies.The basic structures of a human body are a particular kind of idea and in such process, if a deep research has been done then we get that every part of biological body has a knowledge to know; like – a naked individual is sitting somewhere with shut eyes. A girl of young age of 20 years touches his back by his palm the touched back says to the mind of body that this is a hand of young girl. How this process became?

Because every part of body has a memory a knowledge and when a part of body comes in touch or contact of another thing that organ quickly reports to the brain that such kind of contact or touch is here. Then as per need and as according to nature and mood of person his brain orders to other organs like hand etc, to help or support to that organ from which part of body the report was send to mind.

How all this is possible as because of the knowingness, sensiti- veness and security feeling restored already in all parts of body. Thus we get that the whole body is nitted also by the ideological system and knowingness of the things in all over the body. The knowledge is not restored only in consious or subconsious mind. It is often restored or kept by body in all over the biological body with the help of elemental, minute & psychological bodies of an individual. This may be proved in animals too. If some one touches a back of cow by his palm she reacts by that touch whether she is seeing or not seeing to the palm putter.

This Ideological body has many kinds of such factors & ideological bodies in it. These are:- **(i)** Self dependent **(ii)** dependent **(iii)** half dependent **(iv)** Enchroching.

(i) Self dependent Ideological bodies : A few persons are their who are completely dependents of their selves for any kind of ideas & view or knowledge. Because such kind of persons have a very hard layer of confidence. Many times it becomes over confidence and pays negative result. But even then this is a good stage of ideological body. While over confidence creates ignorancy, cruelty and negativities too.

(ii) Dependent Ideological Bodies : A lot of individuals are often dependents of others for ideas like a child. This stage is not so good but if some one has very good wise well wisher such kind of persons are also getting successes. Whose bodies are dependents of others they work by two ways either they talk front to front to that fellow and take help or they are joint with those persons by unseen connections minutely, it is telepathic connection.

(iii) Half Dependent Ideological bodies : A few persons are there who are half dependents. For few matters they are self dependents and for few matters they need ideological helps such kind of ideological bodies are mostly found in all over the world. These bodies are also full with confidence and pleasures but in few cases these are not normal.

(iv) Enchroching Ideological bodies : So strong will power having many Ideological bodies with a heavy support of minute and elemental bodies enchroch to others bodies and they become a problem for others ideological & psychological bodies. Its not a natural stage this is a psychological sickness & disorder.

(v) Substance : All kind of ideological problems sicknesses, weaknesses, enchroching nature and negativity is curable and improvable in positive form by the help of Yoga, studies and by its light practices.

G. Religious Body :

(i) Learnt Religious body (ii) Seen Religious body (iii) Studied Religious Body (iv) Felt Religious body (v) Realized Religious body (vi) Real Religious body (vii) Substance.

As it has been often seen that a few persons, are said by the people that he is a religious person or some one says for his self that I am a religious person. In the same way a few person say that they are religious. Certainly they are religious persons either they are showing to their religiousness or they are really religious like priests, nuns, saints, padaris or others they have religious ideological or psychological bodies inside them and these bodies are of many kind.

(i) Learnt Religious body : In one of religious bodies is learnt religious body which is learnt from parents, priests or masters or from those people who are admitted by a person as a good person and individual believe or faith on them. This kind of religious body enables a lot and to a person gives peace.

(ii) Seen Religious body : By seeing monk, priest, nuns, saints or to other religious persons and their religious activities or functions of religious kind every one becomes effected negatively or positively in all over the world. Such kind of seen memories also create a certain kind of believe and faith by that seen religious bodies are born which help in-courage & faith.

(iii) Studied Religious body : By the religious studies a person can get several religious knowings and such knowings create a systemized religious body with a proper knowledge of religion of any kind of religion. This kind of studied religions of a person create several ideologicated sentimental solutions in a personality. So religious studies for an individual are like a mental & ideological tonic by which a person gets a lot of solutions of his life, real way of human life, peace and encouragements, patience & inner pleasures too. Till the studies he creates a religious personality in his self which becomes a religious body in his biological body. Laterly when he comes in touch & contact of such religious invironment & in religious activities he improves his inner soul.

(iv) Felt Religious body : Often it happens with an individual that he feels many kind of religious feelings due to several circumstances or happenings either by studies or his by own life. Such kind of felt religious bodies live permanently in a person and give a way and energy, courage, peace and confidence of real way. Such body helps in managing other kind of psychological and ideological setup of a person. A few persons who are sentimental and soft hearted they feel much more.

(v) Realized Religious body : Learnt, Seen, Studied and felt invironment of religion exist ever in subconsious mind and a proper religious body starts to come in existence. Subconsious & conscious mind start properly to work insiany tries too an individual gets failure in being real religde religiously in ideological, psychological, spiritual, elemental & also in minute bodies. By that unseen functions of the body by which biological body takes a real natural stage which becomes an idealistic approach. And by that real realizations come to a person.

(vi) Real Religious body : After all above processes the realities of religion and life come front to front to an individual and a stage of real realistic approach of religion & life starts to come in existence inside a biological body as in an unseen personality which is known as a real religious body of a person. Such kind of developed stages are found often in those persons who are realy peace loving, kind, non violent, and god believing.

(vii) Substance : Often it becomes that after mious person and the real peace as well as with devine realizations become unachievable factor to most of the persons. Yoga is the way which is a fast supportive factor for human's life by which several biological, worldly & other kind of many difficulties of feelings & ideas are solved quickly and results come very positive for all kind of lives.

H. Spiritual body :

(i) Self living	**(ii)** Support living	**(iii)** Combined living
(iv) Multi living	**(v)** Weak Spirit	**(vi)** Powerful spirit.

In the human body spiritual body and spirit boath are the cause by which an individual has a life. When these boath leave the body the person dies and with spirit as well as with spiritual bodies the minute and elemental bodies excluding the element of earth water & space go away. Thus the importance of spirit and spiritual bodies is like life and death for a human body.

(i) Self living spiritual body : Often most of the individuals are self confident and self living. Such kind of persons have an independent spiritual body inside their biological body. This kind of spiritual bodies are called self dependent and self confident bodies. Whether these are self confident but their developments & achievements are as in mass peoples achievement. It's a common & general stage of spirit.

(ii) Support living spiritual body : There are a lot of spiritual bodies in human bodies which can not live in their own bodies without any support. So they ever live with a support of another spiritual body's support. As often becomes with the children they cannot live alone in a lightless room in nights. In the same way many -2 soft nature's and very sensitive bodies ever live with support.

(iii) Combined Living Spiritual Body : Yes it's a surprise to know first time that a lot of humans are there who are not living alone inside their own bodies. They have another spiritual body too, in their own biological body. These are called combined spiritual bodies. These another bodies living in some one's body may be dead persons spiritual bodies or alive persons spiritual bodies in a percent to support.

(iv) Multi Living Spiritual Body : A few biological bodies are like a lodge or Hotel or as a house. Many spiritual bodies live there and when they need they go out from the biological body such kind of spiritual bodies who are owners of their biological bodies may be very weak or very strong and successful persons or too much failed.

(v) Weak Spiritual Body : As it is often seen that a lot of personalities are so strong and powerful and others are very weak in comparision of such strong personalities. Many pious or cruel good or bad spiritual bodies are living in biological bodies which are very weak, whether many of them show their selves so strong and powerful but in fact these are very weak. A few common nature's spiritual bodies are also so weak while often it has been seen that many of artists; musicians; literary persons; thinkers; religious persons spiritual bodies are so weak like children of 12-15 years or as like very soft hearted women too.

(vi) Powerful Spiritual Body : A few spiritual bodies are very much powerful they are powerful due to many causes either from past births or from the present birth they have been made theirselves so powerful by religious penance, hard works, good works or by too much negative works & cruelties. Many times such bodies are enhealthen by the atoms of another supernatural power. Such spiritual bodies are not common individuals. Whether they also have a simple biological body as others in which they live. Many times such kind of powerful spiritual bodies are a natural disorder in a biological body.

Substance : If a spiritual body is well then often all kind of bodies and life of an individual lives well. If a spiritual body is normal Yoga helps it to become enhealthen, fresh, devine and more natural and powerful. If a spiritual body of an individual is suffering through any one kind of disorders or many kind of disorders Yoga helps to remove all such disorders from spiritual body and from all kind of bodies of a person. He gets a natural & well stage by the help of Yoga.

I. Behavioral Body:

(i) Human Behaviour **(ii)** Real Behaviour **(iii)** False Behaviour
(iv) frustrated behaviour **(v)** Normal Behaviour **(vi)** Disorders
(vii) Substances.

All kind of psychological factors create a certain kind of behavioral body in a person. And These bodies are being bothered due to the very difficult life of today's era. To know all such behavioural informations it's a need to go through books of psychology. Here as briefing, a few things of behavioral bodies have been written for a basic knowledge of Yoga practitioners. It's a basic thing to know self in Yoga so that when an individual is in practice he may remove the problems & disorders.

(i) Human Behavior : Commonly a human behavior is a component of several psychological factors in itself and since the many decades it is a subject of study of many scholars of psychology. Often behavior is based on some one's personality development. But today the negativity in behaviors has been become a component of personality.

(ii) Real Behavior : It is a very sadfull thing for all humanity & human race that the real behavior of humans by heart and what they are naturally has been reduced too much in percentage. Whether such persons are there, who are living with their real behaviors but the percentage of such people is not more than 40 to 50 percent of the world population.

Due to the fast changes of the social, political, financial lives of the world, human nature, behavior, authentivity and faith has been effected badly.

(iii) False Behavior : In all kind of those business and jobs which are dealed by multinationals are based on the theme of false motivations, that false is for attracting the people towards the purposes of business of such companies. Persons working inside such groups have been practioners of false behavior and others in their contact have also been effected by them and trend of such kind has lost the reliability of individuals.

(iv) Frustrated Behavior : Due to such kind of sentimental breakings, behavioral shocks, failures of ambitions and other a lot of problems a certain percent of Metropolitan cities & big cities persons has been psychologically frustrated and these persons have lost their own targets. Their ambitions they are loosing with their potency and stemna of life struggles. Thus their frustrations are now coming in their own behaviors in all kind of works & in interactions with others.

It is a very sadful stage of individuals. It needs psychological helps.

(v) Normal Behavior : Still a lot of persons are living their lives successfully and they are behaving normally. Still they are living normal and enough natural for normal behavior it is obvious to live natural and psychologically normal. Whether, today it is a difficult stage of living but this is the only fruitfull way of life living.

(vi) Disorders : Due to heavy burdens, social, residential, sentimental, financial, and other kind of insecurities and uncertainties a huge number of world people is passing through the abnormalities either these are very light, light, lightly deep or deep. These are the psychological disorders of normal life which need little psychological helps.

(vii) Substances : Human race is passing today from the very critical, typical and uncertain stages of all kind. In this period deep and stable patience and peace of mind is badly needed to every one. But in todays life there is quite lack of such factors of life. Yoga is the way by which all kind of critical stages an individual may live normal and well.

H. Imaginative body :

(i) Real Imaginations **(ii)** False imaginations **(iii)** Mixed imaginations

(iv) Disorders **(v)** Substance.

Inside a psychological personality of an Individual a very big part is built of imaginations. Such imaginated part of psychological personality is called as imagenative body. Such imaginative body has two kinds, few are real imaginations & others are false imaginations. Excluding these two there is one another of imaginative body that is a mixed part of both the imaginations. When these are imbalanced in a person a third stage becomes that is disorder.

(i) Real Imaginations : Those imaginations which are followed behind the real facts of real life are known as real imaginations. Several plannings of life, many or most of the programmes of works and life are also imaginated by persons. Such kind of imaginative works, plans, programmes are known as real imaginations. Thus it is obviously certified by the life that the imaginations and imaginative part of psychological personality has a big importance without that no one can live his life. Neither the big plans may be planned.

(ii) False Imaginations : Many persons are their in the world who live in imagination world. Their all plannings, all ambitions are being fulfilled inside their imagination world. But they never live its single percent in their own life. All these are false imaginations for them in the words of psychology.

But there is one another fact that is a top secret of human life and human psychology and that is only discovered by the high class yogis and mantrikas only. They can see this secret that those persons who are living in world of false imaginations they are not false. Actually, unknowingly they are imaginating many of these for others and many are there who are unknowingly or knowingly living their imaginations some where in world.

(iii) Mixed Imaginations: In a few persons there is a psychological stage in which they pass from boath the stages of imaginations. For real life they live in real imaginations and for mental rests, they live in false imaginations. Sometimes they live boath kind of imaginations for others. By telepathic attachment and transportations such imaginations are transferred in an other bodies or in masses. Yes it is possible a lot of persons in history have been happened which were changing the society ideologically and sentimentaly by their imaginations. Such kind of mixed imaginative stages are often found in every one but till when these are balanced till then these are easy to live but some times these become abnormal.

(iv) Disorders : Such kind of abnormalties are called disorders of imaginations of a psychological body. These disorders may change a personality in negative or positive boath shapes. This disorder may make a young boy very introvert or a very kind person or may change in a cruel person or in a criminal personality. At least 5 to 15 percent of the humans are passing through such kind of imaginative disorders but they donot knew that infact they are not normal psychologically.

They live in the society but when the time comes their abnormality comes out in their works and they prove that they are cruels, cowards, escapist or others. Such disorders till a limit create no harms but they damage the powers.

Substances : For such disorders a lot of studies are being since last century in psychology and psychological therapists are making well to such people. But it is a therapy in which an individual want to disclose and share his self with therapist. Whether no one likes to share his personal secrets with some one. For such people the Yoga is the best one way it makes all such people normal without disclosing theirselves and gives a new pleased successful life.

K. Psychological Body :

(i) Memories **(ii)** Expectations & hopes **(iii)** Ambitions & wills

(iv) Sentiments **(v)** Feelings & Realizations

(vi) Real life & Psychological Stages.

Psychological bodies of a human body are unseen but are most one important factor of some one's life. If a person is encouraged psychologically he may live a better life. Due to several causes of birth and development a lot of persons are there who are not well psychologically and they feel their lives not so better nor good. What is that? There is a big short coming of psychological development, psychological setup and psychological disorders as well as psychological weakness and they feel discouraged, depressed, fail or weak.

In fact psychologicfal bodies of a human body are just a bunch of several supportive psychological parts of life and these all are naturally nitted inside the biological body with the threads of elemental and minute bodies. In a human life psychology is the only important factor by which an individual goes upto sky in the way of success and achievements. If psychology is weak then life itself becomes a big burden. A very healthy person may be very weak psychologically and another physically very weak person may be so strong psychologically. Who is strong psychologically he is strong and best struggler in life. Memories, expectations and hopes, ambitions and wills, sentiments, feelings & realizations, real life & psychological stages with these six factors we will study the psychological bodies in this chapter. In fact psychology of a human is a subject of total study, which is so big field for studies. But very shortly just for basic learnings and to know the self here a few chapters and points has been written for the purpose of Yoga learners and exercisers of the Yoga.

(i) Memories : (a) Memories of real life **(b)** Memories of false life **(c)** Effects of boath **(d)** Substance.

When child comes in world since then several kind of memories start to store in his consious and subconsious mind and that is his personality. In psychological bodies of an individual about 50% part is full of memories. And 20 to 30 percent part is full of imaginations. The rest part is being used for life by ideas, daily life works, routines, plannings & problems. There are memories of two nature. Many kind of memories in life are never used again or such memories are never going to be happened in life but even then these are existing in psycho-body.

(a) Memories of Real Life : The memories of real life are those memories which are restored in the individuals mind by his own experiences and also those memories are counted in this part which are seen by the individuals. The incidents, works, places, things, journey, taste, sleep, eating, awaking and other life experiences of any kind which have happened in own life or those memories from events seen by the individuals are counted in this part. Such kind of memories give the knowledge and idea of real life to live. So these memories, have big importance in the life of an individual. Because by these memories' a personality develops in a real stage of psychology.

(b) Memories of False Life : A big part of an individual is based on false memories; These false memories are heared incidents or stories, talks etc. Even the studied books are often false memories because the individual has not lived nor faced such things which are spoken in the books. But when such spoken informations in books are experimented in life these memories' few part converts in real memories. One another kind of false memories exists in every one's psychological body and that one is a imaginated saying of about his life. Like a young boy says a false story to his friends whether he says a real story but that story is a false for him because he has not experienced it in real life. This part of memeories creates a weak but creative personality.

(c) Effects of Boath : In today's life & society boath kind of lives are used for success but the effects of boath kind of memories on personality are not same. The real life and its memories are ever fruitfull and stable inside the personality and in psychological bodies. But the false life's memories are not well nor fruitfull in a psychological body. Whether many times false memories are giving big achievements. Such kind of memories of false life and the habits of the false life are never stable. They harm too much to a psychological setup of a person. As because of this fact that once upon a time a period comes in life when such false memories go out and a gap creates which is mental block.

Substance : The real life and its memories enable to a person and his all kind of bodies inherrited in him but the false memories cause big problems inside such bodies. But in today's life it is difficult to count the false memories and the false parts of the life. That's why a lot of persons are passing from big tenstons and stresses because false never may be made a truth. Thus one day every false life goes down and individuals go in depressions and in anxiety or to a stage of anxiety nuronsis. In such cases Yoga is a gift of Indian Rishis. By Yoga an individual can change his life in real life and with all successes he can get a fruitfull life. In other hand Yoga creates all kind of balances and boldness to face the adverse stages.

(ii) Expectations & Hopes - (a) Expectations **(b) Hopes :** In psychological body a person has a lot of complicated gatherings of many many kinds of psychological things. In them expectations and hopes have too much importance. In fact these are hopes & expectations which are creating a future for a person. On the way of hopes &

expectations a person nits his future's life or he plannes his future's life. If these are broken by someone or by circumstances often he becomes nervous.

(a) Expectations : A person expects a lot of things from his parents in childhood if these are fulfilled he is cheerful and if these are not fulfilled he becomes nervous and hopeless many times. If the breaking of expectations is often becoming in one's life really it creates a negativeness in personality and there is a big chance of development of a negative personality as this may create cause of sadistic or aggressive personality. Either it may create a hopeless personality. Expectations are often from much more people than parents and breaking of expectations creates disorders in life & in person.

(b) Hopes : Hopes with life, hopes with self, hopes with plannings, hopes with job, hopes with time, hopes with God, hopes with friends, hopes with family, hopes with friends, hopes of life, hopes with works, hopes with masters, hopes with children, and hopes with all, are causing a structure of future life in a person. Sometimes these hopes are fulfilled as it is and many times these or not fulfilled from the second part as due to many problems of the second part. But whenever these hopes are near to be not fulfilled or breaked, an individual gets a shock. Bearance of such shocks is different in every one and a person may break badly due to this kind of shocks.

Substances : Whenever expectations & hopes are fulfilled easily there is no need to be pleased too much. Neither when these are fulfilled hardly may create an anger or aggressiveness, or hopelessness. If these are broken it's a need to become no aggressive. Never break relations, never so anger, don't be hopeless or aggressive. Be cool and keep patience. By the help of Yoga you can keep psychological balance and pleasures.

(iii) Ambitions & wills - (a) Ambitions **(b)** Wills : In a psychological body ambitions and wills prove the gravity, importance and greatness of personality. Ambitions and wills are the factors by which a life way of a person become concreated for achievements and such persons reach upto the highest points of success. A few persons create or feel no ambitions and another side mass of persons have ambitions but they don't will to fulfill all such ambitions. They ever waite or they are ever afraid of the circumstances. In all such kind of cases the depressed and encouraged psychological bodies of person play a role.

(a) Ambitions : One person has a will of a house & a wife with a good earnings. A few persons are there who don't need all such, they like all that but they don't hope all that as because of their psychological nature because their psychological bodies are not of that nature.

Whether there is a big number of persons who want to go upto sky but they never reach. Because they have ambitions only and their wills never support to do all that to achieve. A few persons are there who are very successful. A few persons are there who are never successful, whether they are very hard workers but they ever live hand to mouth only. All such kind of problems are often due to ambitions. A few are full of ambitions and many persons are in quite lack of ambitions.

(b) Wills : Only ambitions are not a way of success but there is a big need of such wills by which the ambitions may be converted in a real truth of life. And without strong wills no one can achieve the goals and achievements of ambitions only wills are also not the cause but real efforts for achievements of such ambitions are ever needed. It has been often seen that a very intellectual and highly qualified person is quite fail in real life and another normally educated and in many cases an illetrate individual person is too much successful, just due to his hard works, good plans, strong wills and good behavior.

Thus there is another factor of life & personality is that a person who is full of with strong wills, hard works & with good plans may get success in one field easily. And if he tries he is able to get success in several fields. It happens that a person who gets success in one field then in several fields and achieves a lot of achievements in his life.

Substances : With several other kind of psychological factors a real combination & coordination between ambitions is badly needed. But in a big percent there is a quite lack of such combination as because of several other disorders of psychological or other personalities and of other kind of bodies. These disorders, abnormalties, weaknesses are totally curable and positively improvable by Yoga. So Yoga is a life science, life philosophy and life manner.

(iv) Sentiments : (a) Sentiments **(b)** Power of sentiments **(c)** Management of sentiments.

Imaginations, hopes, ambitions, feelings, realizations, wills and sentiments all are having much importance in life. There are several other psychological factors of psychological personality but in them here described parts are the most important for a life, so rest parts of psychology has been left here. By balancing and making healthy to these parts only a psychological personality may be made healthy and pleased. Whether feelings are very near to sentiments but sentiments are stable factor and feelings are incidental waves.

(a) Sentiments : As a person has an idea or view for every thing person, place, relatives and in the same way these all thing have a certain place in a person psychologically too. These psychological sensitive realizations are sentiments. These may be very deep for a person or light in an individual. And his psychological personality is often based on such sentiments. He feels an energy, encouragement with these sentiments. When these inspiring things in a persons are being in disorder in a psychological personality it may harm.

(b) Power of Sentiments : A little child has a sentiment that there is a mother who has all cares for him there is a father who is a security level of him. If they are separated, the child is in big problems till when he is not young enough. And after being young too he is never well psychologically. He ever feels harted his sentiments of parental side. In the same way sentiments are based often in worldly things. Some times these are in God or in deities. If these are in God or in deities he is well because he alone is never alone and he adjusts his self by his self and lives in many disorders due to hearted sentiments shelter of God. But worldly person may go.

(c) Management of Sentiments : Sentiments are a big stemna, paying factor, sentiments are deeply situated in one's personality If sentiments are broken a life may be dispersed within moments or within days because sentiments are real power of a personality. To manage the sentiments it's a big need of knowingness of importance of sentiments in own life means which one is how much precious for someone

A person must sit alone in peaceful place and there he needs to analyse his self and then should manage his sentiments.

Substance : By the way of Yoga the replacement of sentiments, refoundation of sentiments and the removal of deep attachment with the sentiments is easily possible by that a person becomes more powerful for life struggles.

(v) Feelings & Realizations - (a) Feelings **(b)** Realizations : Feelings and realizations of a psychological personality are a real natural process. The status of these may be different in every one. And many times due to low status of feelings and realizations persons become abnormal personalities. A common process in a daily routined life feelings to realizations are the alive natural functions by which a humans decide many things and they live life. By the help of feelings brain is secondary in works. Some times brain may be first. The feelings are more powerful in ladies & in children. Chances of disorders in feelings and realizations are found and often with age it becomes.

(a) Feelings : With each and every incident and moment every one receives the waves of feelings. When he goes some where his eyes see the place brain calculates things latterly but first of all he feels something there. He meets to some one knowingly unknowingly he feels something with him and about him it is the brain which needs an anaysis latterly. Excluding a very few persons this natural process of psychological happening becomes in everyone and this stage is the natural stage. Wonderly nature has given a thing to all lives that is feeling. The feeling is usual as the seeing of the seens is a usual process and at the same moment feelings also come in a person that may or may not be effective or non effective, important or non important but if that process is different then this is a problem. That may be a disorder of feelings. Some persons may feel so deeply something and a few may feel it lightly.

(b) Realizations : Feelings for some thing or person may be real or false but often realizations are real but there is a little chance to realize false realizations and that is confusion.

As a person goes to an old palace. He is alone in some place of palace, suddenly he realizes that there is someone but he is not seeing something. Again he realizes that some one has passed from his right side. He is still not seeing something but in the same moment some murmuring sound comes in his ears – "go out of my palace". Again whispering comes in same way. He comes out and a guard says to him that in that part a soul of a princess is living yet. That realization has happened with many persons. So it has been proved but many realizations are only with particular persons.

Substance : Feelings are a most powerful factor of psychological personality and realization of various kind, are naturally proving process and showing of several unseen existences or other phenomenas due to several happenings of life or incidents this natural process may be disordered or by birth it may is an abnormal stage. For its normalization there may be a need of psychologist. But by the normal Yoga practices that may be normalized or may be made again is a natural order within short periods.

(vi) Real Life & Psychological Stages - (a) Real Life **(b)** Psychological stages

Till the 7th decade and 8th decade of the last century it was not a so fast life of humans and the life was smoothly running in all over the world. But since when the machines & computors came in all fields of life the life came in fastest speed. Due to this, the natural stages of humans have been gotten a fastest change. As because of this change the psychological process of body also have gotten a big change. Feelings, realizations, sentiments, wills, sleeps, rests, behaviour, ambitions and naturality of consious & subconsious brains also have been gotten a change fastly.

Every one lives in tensions several kind of stresses are a past of every one's life and life is being perterved in an unnatural stage psychologically, ideologically, biologically and in other ways too.

(a) Real Life : A lot of needs are now a need of life. To achieve all these every one works hard every one lives in ambitions, keeps wills in mind, runs hither & thither to earn much more. But often most of the persons are not getting all achievements as according to their targets or time. Many kind of sounds are giving tensions; various kinds of insecurities of life are in every life, lack of several needed means are causing a cause of various stresses. Good foods are available but every one can not efford it. All these create a cause of tensions. There are good houses, but they have a big need of enough money. Every one do not can efford such money. It creates cause of tensions. Every where good jobs with very good packages are available but every one is not in such jobs by which they can make their, good worldly life. It also causes tensions.

Every one likes to live with all his family but due to lack of money families are being dispersed fastly. These are also creating sentimental frustrations & insecurity feelings too. High rates & prices of daily life's things are a big cause of problems. About 30 to 40 percent people in the world are passing through too much tensions due to lack of money and rest are passing through tensions due to extra heavy burdens of works and achieving targets. Every where all kind of insecurities are fastly decreasing the powers and stemnas of individuals.

(b) Psychological stages : No believes, no faiths, no truths, no guarantee, no securities, no sentiments, no certainty, no peace, no wills, all such kind of psychological shocks are daily coming to the persons. Every one's psychological nature is life with peace, security feelings family's sentimental support to each other, certain job with enough earnings, a certain residence of his own, a few religious moments, little recreations and then deep sleeps generally it was the life of humans before 3 decades - And human life was peacefully passing every where. It was better than today to live with minimum means. It was better to eat simple foods than today's typical and intercontinental foods.

It was easy to walk on roads by foot. It was easy to go by bicycles. But there was security, there was peace, there was patience, there was certainty, there was satisfaction, there was enough deep sleep, people were with their family and they were well than today. Today after loosing family, peace, sleeps, and every natural stage of human lives people are living in problems, stresses, in tensions and in insecurities too.

By this kind of life how psychological, stages of an individual may be kept well, healthy and natural : A lot of persons are bothering by diseases either these are psychological or biological. They are suffering from the insecurities of that – after this job where they will go, after this month where they will live. All such abnormal psychological stages are every where today.

Substance : In a human body all kind of components are dependents of each other. If one is strong & well it helps and enables to other components. But if one is deeply sick all go to such kind of weakness, if that stage is till the long period.

Today often it is difficult to keep natural to all components. Enviornmental pollutions, lack of means, peace, sentimental frustration, negative responses, every where cheatings, unbelieves, breaking of hopes are damaging fastly to every one. And no one can do same thing against all these circumstances. But it's a need to keep well to all bodies of an individual to live well till the long periods. How it is possible in this era of fast speed. How it is possible? It is very difficult. It is often possible by the deep studies of Yoga and by its practices. Yoga is not merely a bunch of physical exercises but it is a life style, it's an art of life. It's a life philosophy which is comfortable in every era of human lives. ❑

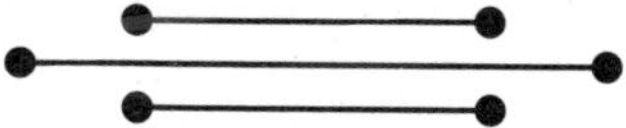

PROBLEMS OF LIFE AND INDIVIDUALS

(a) Life **(b) Problems** **(c) Individuals.**

In fact to which every one knows and says that life is so big & broader. It has several factors, components and problems. After knowing such facts an individual may think & manage his life. As a few persons say 'Life' to their personal life only and they believe that this is life. Whether there are a lot of persons who say life to their self family life; anothers are there who say life to their combined family life (Parental & Self); Others are their who say life to their social life with which they are deeply attached and devoted for that. In the same way a lot of possiblities of meanings of life are there whome peoples are living knowingly or unknowingly.

Thus as the possiblities of variety of life are there the problems of such lives are running with people step to step, day today like a undevidable fact or as a part of life. Here shortly a lot of questions of such lives has been arised and the ways of solutions also have been talked. Here life has been discussed in three parts **(A)** Life **(B)** Problems and **(C)** Individuals. Even the life again has been classified in five parts to make it easy to understand its pressure and to clear its structure in one's mind. These five parts of life are **(i)** self life **(ii)** family life **(iii)** Relative's life **(iv)** society life **(v)** Life of others. The third part of this chapter derives the roles and their situations in all such life parts and that has been described shortly in five headings, these are **(a)** Individulas and self **(b)** Individuals & family **(c)** Individuals & Relatives **(d)** Individuals & Society **(e)** Individuals & others.

The second section of this chapter is a bridging ledder of boath sections which is deriving six headings to clear more and more the real picture of life & its problems, even with the relativity of effects of all such things in one's life on brain, heart and in life too.

A. Life :

(i) Self **(ii)** Family **(iii)** Relatives
(iv) Society **(v)** Others.

Life, life life ...every where in every talk we hear and we talk about life. But when some one says about life – "Now a days it is very much difficult". He might be saying about social life, and other one may be saying for his own life, another one may be saying for his relatives' life or some one may be saying for his family life. That family life also might be having sense of parental family or his own family. So we see that life is a very broader aspect. It's not a single one aspect for which some one may be saying.

Thus the life is a contribution and gathering of several aspects of life it may be about health, wealth, problems, relations, self, family or society.

So to study shortly it has been discussed in five parts to sketch a real structure inside the mind and these are – **(i)** Self Life **(ii)** Family life **(iii)** Relatives life **(iv)** Society's life **(v)** Other's life.

(i) Self Life : Whether in all parts of life some one's self is indulged and facing, enjoying, caring participating. But even then one's self life is a different aspect than other aspects of life. If someone is engaged in many kind of life aspects but his own self life is well then he may participate easily in other's life and may do good for others. But if one's self life is not well it is very difficult to do in a healthy way for others. To live all kinds of life aspects is also a big struggle of life if personal or self life is not good.

There is another kind of possibility. A few persons are there who donot have much more personal lives. They have devoted their lives for others. And when others are in problems, in pains and incomforts they feel 'theirself' in very big problems. But a few persons are there who have much more personal lives and the problems of others or lives of others are not so important for them.

(ii) Family Life : Often every one says for life, talks for life but no hearer may understand that for which life some one is saying. So it's a need to know that which life is important and big for him. Some are deeply devoted for his family life and their 'self lives' are really very little in their own life but family life has much more place. Such kind of persons are every time thinking and doing for their family and for family life only. That is an identity of their life. A big percent of individuals in young generation is their who do not know the sentimental satisfactions of family and they never enjoy the family pleasures, peace and sharings. Really these are so cowardish and missblessed persons of God & nature. But its their life, they do not know that a family support or to support the family gives too much psychological things to a persons. Thus one's family has a real meanings of life in it.

(iii) Relatives life : Excluding the parental family or own family there are a lot of relatives and their families every one has relationshiop with them very weak or so strengthened. A few persons are there who never like the relatives neither inside their parental family nor in his own family they are very conservative, selfish and cowardish persons. They can't bear littlest mental burden of relatives neither they can keep patience and heart for others particularly for their relatives. But this all is not a healthy behavior, Every one has a social circle in which family, relatives, friends & social persons are involved. But who has a very conservative view for others and lives for his self only may be counted as mentally weak and cowardish person. Since the agos human race is living with loveful relations of the relatives. But it may be a botheration & burden many times and that also may cause tensions & problems.

(iv) Society's life : No one can depend on his self only because a lot of needs of a person are being fulfilled by the society & by social persons. As for example every one walks on roads, eats foods, wears cloths & several other things uses which are necessary for life. But all these are not products of self. Such articles are produced by the others. Yes a few persons say I have paid for that. It's not an answer because they are not authentic persons of money. A little small paper of many colours has gotten guarantee by others which is being exchanged in leaue of several things and that is known as currency. This way every one is dependent of society and has social relations. Thus the society life effects to every one who are not aware and care full for society are not normal persons they are mentally sick and they are cowardish. This is a certain kind of disorder.

It is a process of life that every one is sharing society life there may be a difference of percent of investment of time and participation. If some happening happens in some one's surroundings or in country no one could live without its psychological effects. That also depends on persons that how much they are attached.

(v) Other's life : There is no knowing of a lot of persons, either it is a just heared knowing or read knowing from news papers, as some people are not someone's countrymen, nor they are equal professionals but if some thing happens some where in world naturally a human heart and brain comes in effects of such happenings.

Excluding the humans, an example is here a street wandering dog barks ever on some one and one day that dog's one leg becomes injured badly by a four wheeler, at first sight every one feels that it was a bad dog of street he was deserving for this. But after a few moments a human heart feels that it's not a good driving every one must see for other's problems. This dog needs mercy of humans and that one is also passing his life some how inside the society with his good or bad nature & habits. But we are humans we must care for others. Thus in every heart & brain the natural – process of effects of other's life continues but a few persons may take it deeply and some may lightly or may neglect.

B. Problems :

(i) Problems of self **(ii)** Family problems **(iii)** Problems of relatives
(iv) Problems of Society. **(v)** Problems of others **(vi)** Problems of life.

Now when we have been known of the life and its effects we should also know that these problems are not only psychological & till the thoughts. In fact ninty percent of such lives are mortally & physically attached with every one and they need a sharings of a particular person.

Because life is not an unseen or invisible world which may be avoided by an individual. Commonly in life all things are infront of us as a real situation. It goes to a person that what kind of attitudes he has in his mind and what kind of behavior he adopts at the moment of living his share with such lives. And as according to his sharing, behavior, attitude or shortly as according to his own role the particular life may result him in future.

As I know Dennise from Purtgaal she is law student. She goes to work in Holland by the permission of his parents and then comes back she studies and works hard inside his father's fields in which they grow flowers & fruits they also cooperate her.

(i) Problems of Self : As others, every one has a lot of self problems in today's life. But there is a magic of life that how much you solve your problems by your self and how much problems are solved by others. If you have shared well for problems of others people may come to your own problems too and you will not feel alone. This is life where you should not feel hopelss, discouraged, and alone in life psychologically.

A lot of problems your relatives, family persons, society people, friends may solve but for a few problems you may need to struggle by yourself. Thus we see life is a participation – 'do it get it'. A lot of self problems of works, jobs targets, wills, hopes, desires and ambitions are there which are personal challenges of life for which no one other can do excluding those people who are coming in the way of your such targets jobs or ambitions. These problems may be effecting to a person shortly, deeply, heavily, badly or these may encourage too.

(ii) Problems of Family : As it has been talked that problems of life, sharing the life, effects of life & what are the effects of life of others in some one's own life. That is first of all practically as a problem to which sharings & participations are needed. It's another thing that what happened after the problem. How an individual treated the particular problem and what its result was practically then what the family felt for the person?.

There is a big field of problems, needs, happenings these may be big or little, deep or light, long or short. The family may or may not need you to participate. But if one participates in each need then naturally he becomes a good family member. And he becomes a need of family. All family members may keep hopes with that person and that fellow wins over the hearts of all. Problemss are never so difficult but difficulty is in view that one takes all these. In other hand there are a lot of individuals now who never wish to help, cooperate, participate or to please the family. Such people may feel well to their selves but in fact the are loosing a lot that may not be counted.

(iii) Problems of Relatives : As there is family of parents or some one's own in the same way there is a big role of relatives in some one's life, either it gives a lot of sentimental loosings or encouragements. Some times practically the big helps or shocks are gotten from relatives. Thus relatives are also very undividable part of life which have to exist till the life. Effects, relations, sharings, helps, sentiments, coordinations may be short-long, deep-light good or bad. Many times self family and parental family becomes secondary and relatives with their families become primary for one's life. That depends on circumstances.

But it's a fundamental believe of each country & every society that than the social persons, their families & relatives and their families are better reliable persons. Many kind of cheatings & frauds may be avoided due to the sharings & participations of relatives & their families. Shortly how much one participates and becomes effected it goes to relatives & persons as well as with circumstances.

(iv) Problmes of Society : Noice, crowd, quarells, drugs, accidents, crime, illiteracy, electricity unavailability of necessary means there are several problems like all these. Postering onwalls, keeping dogs and creating problems, children of others, vehicles of others, nonsense behaviors of others, spiting, smoking of several other kinds may be listed like job problems, less payments for hard works, lack of good foods in a town hotels, lack of good teachers for children in school's etc.

All such problems are directly or indirectly being faced by every individual in daily life and in life of long ways but one can couldn't do alone for all such. There may be a few individuals who may agitate the people against all such problems or they may attract the attentions of Govt. towards all such but every one can't. Thus the effectivity of society problems may be assessed on own level too.

(v) Problems of other ; Dogs don't mean the only subject of this heading whether previously one example was there. Problems of others means any problems of society, is a part of society. And because every one is a part of society so every one comes in contact or in effects of problems of others as for example every one is not a user or car and bykes but every one is being effected of such pollutions created by these vehicles as well as by bykes too.

Same way every one is not using airconditioners but the whole world is facing the problem of sun heats more temperatures and direct sun rays on earth due to breaking of ozon layer which is caused by the air conditioners converted gasses carbon mono oxide. Every one is not a politician but their decisions are creating causes to be effect for every one. Like no one has harmed terrorists but every one is insecured due to these people. As these all very much possiblities are their which are effecting in many ways.

(vi) Problems of life : Whether all such are the problems of life but in these problems there are a lot of problems which are not directly in many individuals lives. So those problems which are not directly effecting in one's life couldn't be counted as life problems of particular person. Only those problems which are directly effecting to a person are life problems of a person. Whether the world is a world of problems too and every one comes in fields of such problems. Every one becomes a participant of all such but even then only a few problems are one's life problems which have a big mening for a person and these effect, motivate to a person.

Like a few big family problems may effect to family life and to an individuals life, a few social problems may effect badly, a few problems of relatives may need participation necessarily neither it's not possible to meet all such problems to a person. In another hand without facing these problems a person's involvement may be in these and effects may be heavily creating pressures, tensions and stresses to someone because psychologically he becomes indulged.

Substance : Thus the life and its parts must be known and analysed by a person time to time or with a certain gap of periods. It may be said periodically. With the analysis of such life parts and their stages every kind of problems of these parts must be analysed.

When these boath are revised well, then the participation of self and the need of participation must be analysed as according to self and as according to, other's view- like family members, guardians and in case of relatives the view of relatives must be known. Many times due to lack of capability a person gots failure then he must try to become capable and after due to lucher or poor view about all such, persons get failure whether sentimentaly they are attached deeply with all.

Often only honourable, polite, good words give satisfactions and others need only these lovefull words nothing else. But a few very unlucky persons are their who ever fail to please others only by their words. And thus they create a lot of tensions, heart breakings for their selves and for related persons too. It goes towards psychological disorders.

C. Individuals:

(i) Individuals & self **(ii)** Individuals & family **(iii)** Individuals & Relatives **(iv)** Individuals & Society **(v)** Individuals & others.

In fact an individual is very alone in life. We has a lot of relations in society from family to social fields. So he feels encouraged and well. Neither it is often quite impossible to live the life. Only a few persons are there who are living with very minimum relations with others and in them only a few persons are their who are ever well neither after such people go in depressions and in other kind of psychological problems.

Just know an individual it is a need to know his total structure and it is a knowing of self for a person. So here shortly five headings about the life of individuals has been described very shortly. Here discussed facts & possibilities are only a way to think. All these are total facts of an individual's life these may shortly differ person to person.

(i) Individuals & Self – Many persons are their who like to self life. For self only they like to do, to earn, to spend, to walk, to tour, to eat, to lodge, to cloth, to enjoy and to reach upto highest heights of achievements. But they don't share or enjoy all these with family, relatives or with others excluding their very close friends. Even a few are there who don't like to share with friends too. But most of the persons feel their self life, they live it participate with others too. In all such kind of possibilities a person ever feels his self life in botherations and in short comings, in problems, in tensions or in stresses. Whether a few may enjoy all such problems.

This self of a person is too much important and very meaningful which enables a person to struggle the life struggles. Many times the stages of self become so weak and poor and due to that an individual may really become weak in his real life. So every one should care for it.

(ii) Individuals & Family : Many times individuals alone are nothing, their existence is based and dependent of their family. But severals are their who are failed to please their family persons. They know their rights but they never know their duties. They never please neither by their selves nor by others. If all family members talk such people with love, gently, politely then too they show their aggressiveness, rudeness, and cruelty by worlds and behavior. How such people may live pleased and may keep lived please to their family persons. While family donot need much more means or money to please or to live pleased. Certainly it's a need and natural, social, moral, human & religious duty of everyone to satisfy the parental and personal family by best behavior. A few very selfish nonsense and cruel persons ever pain to their family persons by their behavior. These are mentally poor & psychologically very sick persons. How much reliable companionship is found inside the family now where it is. But some times it gives pains & strains too.

(iii) Individuals & Relatives : Second reliable companionshiop and coordinations are existing inside the relatives, If the good pleasant & eneough relations are kept continuously. Relatives also give an encouragement, psychological support, confidence and other cooperations. So its a need to keep their relations well. Many persons have no relatives, and alot of persons are their who have no relations with their relatives. A few very unfortunate persons are their who have very painful relations with their relatives due to several causes & circumstances, which may bother till all over life to them and may cause stressess.

(iv) Individuals & Society : Many times persons are totally dependents of the society people for their all works, to share the pains & pleasure, for needs and supports. It happens with them who are totally cut of from their families and a few circumstances are also there in which individuals have no relationship with the persons of society. They don't give and take to social people or they donot share pains and pleasures with the persons of Society. This stage is also not so well upto a certain limit every one should have relationship with Society people it also enables many times to a persons. But there are certainties that botheration & stressess upto a limit have to come from there too.

(v) Individuals & others : The last possibilities of relations & dependencies of life are in others and without any direct cause as others may give several supports like a Taxi Driver serves, a Hotel serves, A Barber serves and releases the tensions and problems. In the same way they or that kind of persons who are causes of problems or things; behaviors of such people may create pains & problems although an individual has no relations with them as like neighbours may bother, persons where an individual is working may become big cause of tensions. Some times good adjustments with others become a cause of encouragement, peace and support. But many times they become a cause of tensions, stresses, botherations, dippressions and disorders of psychological setup. All such effect to one's life.

Substance : A lot of possibilities of life and problems has been shown in this chapter so that the persons who are passing through several problems, stresses, tensions and dipressions or other kind of abnormalities may analyes their selves and may keep balance in their lives. But actually, all such sayings of life & individuals are for this purpose that the very old and tight knoughts of life and mind can be made loose and they may liberate their selves from such knoughts of life. If it is not possible by self to make up self then Yoga may help psychologically, biologically and by all kind, real healths and powers may be achieved for life struggles. ❑

YOGA

Kinds of Yoga :

(a) Karmayoga	**(b) Bhaktiyoga**	**(c) Sanyas Yoga**
(d) Mantrayoga	**(e) Sankhya Yoga**	**(f) Prem Yoga**
(g) Kriya Yoga.		

In fact Yoga is a science, art and management of body by which an individual lives his life and achieves a lot of achievments. If that body is well till the long periods and is strenghtened by a few special powers mental, psychological, biological, elemental & spiritual, the individual may exist well in this world than others. So keep well the body. This book of Yoga is authered to achieve better powers of life, to keep and attain best attitudes and ways of life. But to attain all such achievements of Yoga obviously it was a big need to know the human body well. Shortly and synopsisly that has been narratted in a few chapters and I believe that the learners and Masters & Scholars of Yoga will get a new scientific view from this book and Yoga will pay them a lot than previously. Yoga has a lot of fields here shortly a few Yogas are being synopsised for information.

A. Karma Yoga :

As there are Bhakti Yoga, Sanyas Yoga, Prem Yoga for Bhaktas & Saints or for vanaprasthas. In the same way another Yoga way is there and that is known as Karma Yoga. This Yoga is for (Grihasthas) means for worldly & family people whoose working for life, to live alive.

Properly with a certain nonviolentic way to work with justice with full devotion and with full mental powers is known as Karma Yoga. In Geeta it has been said that the expertness of Karma (works) is Yoga. By the way of Karma a person may get peace and pleasure. Because earth (World) is Karm Lok (The world of works) so this Yoga is depending on Karma by that too God & normality may be achieved.

B. Bhakti Yoga :

Faith, believe, devotion and love with God or on some Deity is Bhakti. Live the worldly life with a deep faith and devotion on God. So sit with saints and with religious people to learn the way to reach to the God or to your selected deity. Know the all things about the God and go in deep stages of such devotion. You do worldly works for living without any attachment in world and faith on God for result. Every time repeat the names of God or mantra of your deity. What the God will like better for you, he will do it for you, be satisfied in that, don't loose your patience. Live in minimum means and trust on God or on your deity. This is Bhakti Yoga. Live with patience, peace and with devotion God. Don't be devoted in world. Don't live with attachments in world or in worldly relations, all these are for short periods and God is ever existing, so love the God. Before your birth and after your death only God will care for you. So trust on him. Live with non-violence, justice and peace. Live with devine feelings and sentiments. All worldly problems will become solved automatically.

C. Sanyas Yoga :

In this world several kind of attachments, liabilities, duties, and ambitions, wills, expectations are causes for which a person does works all the life and becomes bothered all life. Just to get free own life from all kind of such botheration there is a way leave all that. No work, no relations, no liability, no money, no house, no duties, no attachments, no works, no results and no worldly life. Go in shelter of God devotedly. He will give a chance to you, he will help you. He will care for you. Live with a way of real Religous and Spiritual knowledge.

Leave the Karma and leave the results of Karma. You will live free from all kind of problems. This is said Sanyas Yoga. Its an Indian way of life. Become a Saint (Sanyasi). Live on the dependency of God become total dependent of God. No worldly attachment is needed. Don't Keep a single or minutest feeling or attachment in world live free with deep knowledge of God and realize the God in all things every where.

D. Mantra Yoga :

As according to the many Yogas the another prominent Yoga is Mantra Yoga. By the repeatition of Mantras an individual may get several things. This is the way by which worldly, non worldly, spiritual, religious and supernatural achievements may be achieved within short periods. A lot of Mantras are there which are having powers to give money, a lot of Mantras are there which are having power to give wisdom. And there are millions of Mantras of several veriety by which an individual may achieve any kind of expected things. Yes Mantras have a very vider scope of life.

There are two Yogas ashtaang Yoga and Mantra Yoga which are giving every expectations fulfilled by its practices. Garuntedly, Yoga gives the real results. By the way of Mantra Yoga the way of God is also easy to reach. By Mantra Yoga a person may Liberate himself from all botherations and may achieve all achievements and may live normal too.

E. Saankhya Yoga :

Saankhya Yoga is another kind of Yoga. By this a person can liberate his self from the worldly attachements, tensions and from all pains which is comming in life daily. Just with a little practice of a half an hour daily, an individual may live peacefully upto 24 hours. After continuous practices of long periods may be liberating his self for all times to his self. By this Yoga also individuals may get quick results. Every kind of abnormalities of brain, stressess & tensions go out within short periods. Peace, patience, pleasure, naturality comes and biological body also becomes fit. Saankhya Yoga is described in Geeta and Lord Krishna has said it to Arjun and several other Yogas have also been said in Geeta. So it should be a need for a Yoga practioner to go through Geeta at least two three times. Saankhya Yoga removes evil and negative things. It restores positive & devine factors by which an individual becomes all devine gradually.

F. Prem Yoga :

There is a real thing that is love, which may be kept all the times for every one because every life and every creation is created by the God. All things, all creations are existing in God. Every creation is a part of God. So Love to all such things. Every moment every person, animal, littlest life, plants, elements and materials are really by God and they are a shape of God different to each other. All such creations are not merely creations but in all these different shapes God it self is existing on the earth. So live with love for all. Love is a virtue, Love is way to reach to the God, to please the God and to built a society. That's why by Prem (Love) has been taken as a mean or way of Yoga. Prem is a Yoga in it self. Many many kinds evil moods, habits, thoughts, negativities go away on the way of Yoga and in the same way the Prem Yoga also reaches upto the God and gives normal life.

G. Kriya Yoga :

As the several Yogas are there which are giving the normal lives and peace to individuals, in the same way Kriya Yoga also solves a lot of problems of a person and gives the peace, normal psychological behavior as with natural stages. This Yoga also gives a way to individuals by which people may reach upto the God and positivity in life comes easily.

Substance: A lot of Yoga ways are there and these all are the ways of life. These all Yogas are life styles and life philosphies. Which give power to live in world with peace, patience, potency, pleasure and devine environments. Yoga gives spiritual health & Power; Yoga makes one's personality Religious pious & natureal. Yoga gives stemna, potency & patience. Yoga reaches upto God. Yoga pays super naturality to a person. Yoga gives worldly life's positive powers. Yoga pays several other human virtues to a person. Hidden powers of person awake and a person becomes better by Yoga. ❑

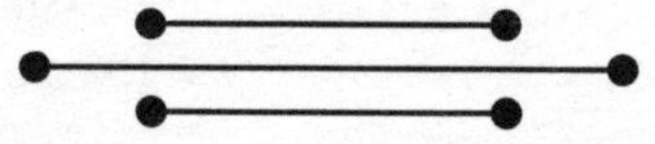

PEARL

PARTS OF YOGA

(a) Yam (b) Niyam (c) Aasan

(d) Pranayam (e) Pratyahar (f) Dhaaranaa

(g) Dhyaan (h) Samaadhi.

The world visible and invisible boath have two qualities - goodness & evils, attraction and welfare. Most of the things are very much attractive in this world but these are not in welfare of individuals in their results. But then too these are very attractive. Many things which are not attractive even these are too much boaring but these are giving good and welfaric results.

How that classification may be noted by a person that which one is harmful in results and has no long roots of future and which is ever good. That may be learnt from Yoga, Yoga books, Yoga scholars and Yoga teachers.

Yoga teaches such lesson and restructures, redesigns, remanages the life for the welfare of all not only for particular human nor for human race only. It sees the welfare of all as welfare of all Lives, natures and welfare of all components of life & all components of nature. There are two kinds of nature of God powers one goes towards ends, ruins & evil another goes towards goods, virtues as well as towards God saves to people from sins & evils that may be non attractive and slightly difficult but in results this is so sweet.

There is an invisible struggle in between boath kind of powers since the creation is created. But a few persons in long past eras realized such facts and they did researches by several methods for life and for welfares of all. They gotten surprising results. This resultive mode is designed in Ashtaang Yoga philosphy.

Join the devine zone start to walk on devine way of God you will get successes and helps in that way. Leave the evil things, evil habits, evil behaviors you will be liberated from the surroundings of evils. When you will come in the way of goodness you will walk in the way of life and God.

Here the whole philosphy of Yoga is not possible to describe in short. But the way of yoga, walked by an individual describes automatically in the way, practically to a person. Thus we may know goods & evils practicallyby Aashtaang Yoga. Good & Evils boath are mixed in the world. but their results are ever existing inside different two kind of things & deeds. Good things and good deeds are having good results as well as bad things and bad deeds are having bad results.

Whether every one is doing the deeds good deeds in his knowledge and wisdom. But how it may be certified that what kind of deed will give which result. There is no problem of it. Yoga already has researched to each and every thing. So without any hesitation one can run on the way of Yoga. It's a very big quality of a good way that a person ever gets good, either minimum or maximum. So why not to walk on the roads of Yoga by which all time welfares may come in life for all. It's another thing that one will enlight the world like a candle and another may enlight the whole world like great persons.

Such struggle of negativity and postivity effects the life and nature every where. Its an invisible process but it is continuing. Only a few percent people may understand this fact. Whether every one is passing from the roads of life. A few part of Yoga philosphy has been decided and designed in life principles exercises and another part has been designed in physical exercise part so that a combination and balance may continue in life and best results to a person may come ever.

Yam, Niyam, Dharana, Pratyahaar are philosphical more than physical and rest are pure physical by which the philosphical part of Yoga is achieved and meets of God become possible. Whether the philosphical part's exercises are achieving the physical & philosophical boath results after complition. In the same way first one also achieves boath. In words of Yoga these eight parts of Yoga are devided in two parts one is Bahirang (Outer Parts) and another is Antarang means inner parts of Yoga. As in new way it has been described that from Yam to Pratyahaar these are philosphical parts and rest are the outer parts of Yoga.

A. Yam :

(i) Ahinsaa (Non violence), (ii) Satya (The Truth),
(iii) Aasteya (No thefting), (iv) Brahmcharya (Completely sex avoiding),
(v) Aparigraha (No collection).

In Ashtaang Yoga philosphy total life, its management and inner-outer designs have to remanage and redesign as according to a new philosphy of life. This new designing of life is not new it is so ancient. Before thousand years it was presented by several scholars and Rishis & Saints of India. They were known as Yogi. but these Yoga philosphies are based on obsolute facts of life, nature and God. Here Yamas are just a part of that philosphy. But this Yam part is a basic theoritical part on which the Yoga philosphy exists. All kind of research works of life, nature and God were designed for comming agoes of future as well as with the present of that time. Because these values are never old and worthless so these are still relevant for human life. We should know that the power is existing on boath sides in Goods and in Evils in positivity and in negativity too. Yoga joints a person to a sector or zone of goodness & positivity. Yamas are as same for that way.

(i) Ahinsaa (Non violence) : For Ahinsaa Maharshi has said that (Ahinsaa Pratisthayam Tat sannidhah vair tyagah) Patanjali.

By body, by words, by thoughts not to pain some one is Ahinsaa (Non violence) To see and to do the evils of others is also a violence. By any method to harm, to kill, to pain is violence. There may be a lot of means to pain some one and to leave all such methods for ever is non violence.

It may be that unknowingly some one might be paining to some one. Now, because that is being by some one, so the liability of such violence goes to painer but that is intensionless may so be excused. Till when a littlest violence is living inside the body and in thoughts and in wills no proper results may come to a practitioner of non-violence. When non violence in a persons life comes completely by practice it gives a lot. The moment comes when non-violence becomes a siddhi in a person. By the Siddhi of non violence every one leaves his foeshiop even if that is natural like deer & lion that also goes away in presence of such Yogi.

(ii) Satya (Truth) : Satya Pratishhayam Kriyaafalashrayatwam - Patanjali.

Maharshi says that by the following of truth in words and in life one kind of Siddhi also comes to a person. By that result of Satya (Truth) a person may give the results to a person who has done a work. Even those results to a person whose are not results of done works of him may be given to some one by that practitioner of Yoga. It means a person who is a practitioner of Satya (Truth) may cause to some one to give results of the works and of no works, means he may create causes in this universe for benefits of a person. By the practice of truth a person may clean his all kind of personality and he may also become eligible person to come in contact of deities. Many times he may change the times of results of one's deeds as a result of some work is going to come in late future days that may be changed slightly nearer in future. Which deed of person is going to give him punishments that result may be changed in prize & honours. Even several other too.

(iii) Aasteya (No thefting) : For Aasteya Maharshi has said -

Aasteya Pratishayam Sarvaratno Pasthanam - Patanjali.

Steya means thefting and thefting spirit, thefting wills, thefting nature. Aasteya means no thefting, no thefting wills, no thefting nature, no thefting spirit, no thefting behavior, No thefting ideas. Really it is very very difficult to life. Firstly see thefting - other's things, money and properties to stole, either by force, by decieving, by fraud or by any wrong way to get is thefting - To stole state properties and finance is also thefting. To take several shares in govt. project & in company projects is also thefting. To take money or something to give govt. releaf and justice is also thefting. A lot of theftings are in human practices today. To leave all such is no thefting.

To depend on parental properties and sum if all that was earned with a totaly justified way and to depend on that money or earning which are earned by own justified effords are unthefted, justified and pious, So ever to depend on pious earnings and not to suggest an ideas to others for several theftings is the following of no thefting (Aasteya).

Thus who some one follows this devine and human principle of life he achieves a sight, a special - a very special sight, a super natural sight by which he can see the Ratnas (Gems) like diamond etc. hidden inside the earth. There also he needs a real. 'No thefting' neither power of seeing (Gems) Ratnas will go away. Even several problems may come after taking that store of Ratnas (Gems).

(iv) Brahmcharya (No Sex) : Brahmcharya Pratisthayaam veeryaalaabhah - Patanjali.

Sex is known by all but no sex means Brahmcharya is not completely known by all. To leave physical sex, mental sex and the contacts of opposite sex individuals with the view of sex, conver satins of sex, thoughts of sex, and to see such opposite sex individuals in such stages all is sex.

So to avoid all kinds and ways of satisfying the sexual sentiments & wills and feelings is the no sex. To touch, to talk, to see, to think, to imagine is totaly prohibitted even such seens, photo, paintings, literature is also prohibitted. Thus, if till the long period such practice is continued then the all kind of powers of body and soul come. That also enables and gives seaman & strength. But if practice is breaked once then again its a need to restart the practice from zero. Whether in second round of practice one may achieve the same stage earlier than the first time's practice. When No sex continues upto years a person gets, feels & realizes a lot of powers in him due to more sex, due to regular sex, due to sexual imaginations, due to sexual thoughts, due to continuous and regular meetings with opposite sex person with a sentiment and thought of sex makes a person weak. Every one looses several natural powers. By the following of principle of no sex a person can recoverer his all loosen powers again and may get new powers too. Even he may get healthy and long life too.

(v) Aparigrah - No collection : For aparigrah Maharshi Patanjali has said -

Aparigrahast hairyei Janmkathantaa Sambadhah - Patanjali.

It means for selfishness or for self luxurious life to collect much more money, to collect countless luxuries, unnesesarily and several other things is known as parigrah (collection). So one should not collect much more money, much more luxuries excluing the needed money and luxuries for life. It doesn't mean not to keep necessities. A worldly person and a family person must keep enough money and things so that he and his family may live better.

But if some one is following the all words of Marshi Patanjali and takes decision to follow all these in any circumstances, in every place at every time; then results of Aparigraha he will get surely by practice. Maharshi Patanjali has said that if some one is totaly following Aparigraha he will know the causes of his all births, gradually, because this is not the only birth of a person. Since last long agoes a person who is a soul only is taking births due to several causes.

And by following a parigrah it is certain to know his causes of birhts. But it is process, with in a day nothing is possible. As an exerciser becomes well, he gets such super natural stages of knowings for hidden secrets of his life. Not only this many ways of other kind of knowingness may come gradually to him by which that he may improve his life and others lives too. This is known as siddhi of aparigrah principle.

B. Niyam :

(i) Shauch **(ii) Santosh - Satisfaction,** **(iii) Tap -Penance,**

(iv) Swadhyaya - Study & Analysis, **(v) Eeshwar Pranidhan - Devotion on God.**

Like Yamas there are five Niyamas these may be said rules. As Yamas are principles of Yoga in the same way Niyamas are the rules of Yoga. These boath are the practices of philosphical part of Yoga by which one's inner personality becomes redesigned and restructured in a real devine life philosphy. That washes the personality as well from inside and reaches upto the outer personality. But the experimental part Aasan, Pranayam, Dhyan etc. starts from physical body and reaches upto the inner soul This all is a certain kind of learning and restructuring of a personality with boath of the ways.

There are five Niyamas which control a person to react in a negative way by such Niyamas an individual invests his all energies in a creative way and learns to practice it to keep the patience till the life as well as with the belive & faith of God. He goes fastly towards the zone of God and gets the several Devine stages and powers with love of God.

(i) Shauch : To win the attachment and attractions of self & others body this is the best one exercise for a yoga practitioner. Maharshi Patanjali says for shauch (Cleanness - Piousness).

Shauchaat Swaang Jugupsa Parair Asansargam - Patanjali.

It means - Shauch - the cleanness the piousness. All kind of cleanness creates a piousness in mind and in sentiments gradually the dirty feelings, dirty sentiments, dirty behaviors go away and the attachment or deep attachments with self body also become so light. The attractions for others body also goes erased but this result may come in many rounds or after a long period of practice.

Satva shuddhi sanmanasyai kagreyendri jayaatmadarshan yogya twaanicha - Patanjali.

Satva : means the inner most elements. Cleanness and piousness gives a lot of benefits in body and in personality. It restructures the nature of the practitioner. After a complete practice someone's inner becomes pious due to which self body attachment decreases & goes away; Secondly the attraction of others bodies also decreases and goes away, thirdly the peace, devineness and natural pleasure with devine pleasures comes inside. Fourthly the concentrations, deep concentrations come in life and instability goes away in place of that stability takes place.

Fifth is the total control on all kind of wills and organs comes. Sixth ability of self realization and the ability of realizing and facing self comes. Laterly, the day comes when a person comes front to front to his self.

(ii) Santosh - Satisfaction : Santoshaadanuttam sukh laabhah - Patanjali.

Maharshi patanjali says that the satisfaction in every stage in every circumstance and in every result, in every moment is the best one stage of a person by which person gets the benefit of uncomparable pleasures. Its a real fact that a person firstly gets a stage of such pleasure realization and then to live in such stage without no means or with minimum means.

Then after as according to his fate, deservation, ability or as according to the world soul, according to the recomendation of nature or as according to the results of his previous deeds, as according to the deities and as according to the mercy of God he gets such pleasure & such devine pleasure for future with or without such means and circumstances. But if one is continuing the practice of cleanness & piousness in all kinds of his deeds, the sins may be won over by him and new possibilities of new circumstances to continue such stage and to get all such uncomparable means may be created. For that deep regular practices are must. But results are sure as according to the Maharshi Patanjali's words.

It has happened with millions of Yogis and Yoga practitioners so it may never be doubtfull some one's practices might be having some short comings in them and by that results periods and modes may slightly differ.

(iii) Tap - Penance : Maharshi Patanjali has said about Tap (Penance) that

Kayendriya Siddhi rashuddhi kshyaata pasah - Patanjali.

It means by the penance body and all organs become pious and a stage of their natural devine power comes in stage of Siddhi (Extreme stage).

Now what is the penance. First of all works (justified) needed for life to do and to bear its pains, difficulties and problems, with patience. To bear all those pains, difficulties which are comming to follow all humanatarian works for others or for nature & society. All those pains and problems to bear in keeping well to family and other close persons.

Then after all those problems, pains and difficulties which are comming in the way of religious activities & practices of own parental or adopted religion like fast, prayers, social services, studies, to serve worship place, to serve the God or to its servants or to serve pious persons, saints, hermits etc. To bear all such kind of problems & pains peacefully with deep patience is known as penance. Thus after knowing penance one should keep continue this practice with faith without any excitement till the long periods. When all such deeds are being completed peacefully several kind of reformation goes in body and in other organs. By these reformations the whole body goes towards piousness and starts to restore the devine energies. When nature needs that also pays, the several powers in body as Siddhis (the extreem stage) which are not in normal persons. These may be as hearing power of world's any conversation and sounds from any place, seeing power of past, present and future, smelling power of world's any smells from any where, touching power to any one from world's any place. This may be from a long distance from object. In the same way this practice gives a very special power to read some one's mind and to convince or order to any one from any where. So Yoga is said that it's not a magic but it works like magic.

(iv) Swadhyaaya - Study & Analysis of self and of his Deity - Swaadhyaadishtdevtaa Samprayogah - Patanjali.

Maharshi Patanjali has said that by the Study & analysis of self & of his God or Deity a Yogi gets front to front the God and to his Deity. In this way, we see that only Yam & Niyam complete the targets of a human life and Yoga too. This theoritical and philosphical part of Yoga and its practices of life principles reaches upto the God and Yoga ends here, by this road. But the another way of physical exercises is rest to work, so that the achievements of this road may live permanently in a person till the long periods. In fact the philosphical exercises of life principles are to create real eligibility of Yogi in a person (Yogi = Yoga Practitioner). After that physical exercises complete the way of Yoga.

Swaadhyaaya means study of authentic religious books, repeatition of Mantras, and thinking of all these as well as with the thinkings of self and God or Deity also. By this practice the next part of life principles practice becomes easy, so it may be said as pre-exercise of eashwar pranidhaan. Whether it is also a complete exercise in it self. By this practice the choosen & worshipped Deity's meet or achieving completes. So this practice is also too much important. When all kind of mal thoughts, evil sentiments and behaviors go out by previous practices of foresaid principles then this exercise works fastly and the Siddhi of this stage comes. By the Siddhi of Deity the virtuous & powers of such Deity come in practitioner and he becomes very special.

(v) Eashwar Pranidhaan - Devotion on God : Maharshi has said about the Eashwar Pranidhan.

Samaadhi Siddhi reeshwar pranidhaanaat - Patanjali.

Eashwar Pranidhan means total dependency on God, to trust on God, to think on God & complete devotion on God. By the dedication on God and totally depending on God the faith comes, an individual starts trust on him and then God helps him. By this practice whether outer world of a person goes in avoidence but inner world joins the zone of God and laterly to God.

Maharshi Patanjali has said about the result of this Eashwar Pranidhan that if the Eashwar Pranidhan is in a complete stage in a Yogi then automatically a person goes in Samadhi stage. Samadhi pays devine feelings realizations and devine life in this body although this Samadhi may be light or deep as according to the devotion.

One another benefit comes in life of Yoga practitioner by this exercise that all kind of life problems and difficulties of Yoga go away by their selves. Because due to total dependency on God, God itself solves the problems of that Yogi. With such kind of Eashwar Pranidhan practice a person leaves all his problems on God and God really manage all such. By the carings of God the other stages of Yoga also go sound and perfect. So this exercise is most important more benefitial and rest paying as well as with the joining of God & devine sector. In other hand by this practice a person performs his duty of being a child of God. This way Yogi remembers ever to him and pleases him.

Substance : Now the one phase of Yoga ends here with the exercises practices & siddhis of life principle exercises of Yoga philosphy. By Yoga philosphy the total development of inner personality reaches upto here and the next phase of Yoga will start in coming headings. Whether Yoga has a complete design but if some one has completed only this phase it is also enough for a life of an individual for development of a good religious and humanitarian personality. It also reaches upto God. It also gives several Super natural and Surprising powers to a person. It also gives devine realizations and devine things. It also makes humans able to meet God.

But the next phase is more physical and it gives better biological and physical achievements. the reachings of next phase are also upto the God.

Which Samadhi is here for Short periods that Samadhi in next phase is for long periods because with a few other kind of exercises the ability & capability of Samadhi increses for hours and for more long periods.

C. Aasana - Sitting.

Sthir Sukhamaasanam - Patanjali.

Aasan is an important part of Yoga. And today most of the Yoga - Teachers are concentrating on Aasan. Whether Aasan is not the only meaning of Yoga but even then it is the basic physical exercise in the Yoga way. Aasan has two meanings. One Aasan means that mean (article) on which he has to sit like mat, blanket, cottonsheet, floor, bed or others. These must be comfortable as the exerciser may sit till the long period without any pain and problem. That should not be so soft neither so hard.

One more thing in Aasan must be cared that is (Nirvighnataa). The place must be full of natural air & natural lights (Sunlights/Moonlights) No one and nothing should be disturbing at the time of exercise. Another most important thing is there that the exerciser must be mentally prepared, his concentration should be only on exercise. So the time, place & circumstances must be already analysed and then choosed.

Aasan Siddhi : Prayatna Shaithilyanant Samapatti bhyaam - Patanjali.

For Aasan Siddhi Maharshi has said - It means by stability it becomes Siddh. Now the kind of sitting and other Aasanas are a subject to work. First of all this thing must have to keep in mind that there are Eighty Four Aasanas and all these may not be described shortly here. Here only one Aasan is being said for the practitioners. And that is Sukhaasana which is said by Maharshi Patanjali.

By several different Aasanas several kind of physical, biological, psychological and devine achievements may be gotton or achieved but by Sukhaasana all kind of achievements are possible within short periods. Sit on a comfortable place in comfortable mean at a comfortable time with a comfortable mood. Then sit constantly without any movement no fingers no hands no neck no eye, should be doing movement. Fix yourself on any one thing. Keep strait your back bone and see one thing only or shut your eye lids. Try to make normal your breaths as easily they may do their in & out. Continue it upto 10 to 15 minutes. Take a little rest and take a few long and short breaths then again do the same upto 10 minutes. Do it daily. After a few weeks or a few days you will realize that you and your body needs not too much movements. You are right this is the one result of Aasan.

When a body leaves unnecessary activities and sits without any movement the all organs get rest body, brain, heart all come at a point of realization and that is peace which is the power of a person. Peace is the divine virtue, peace is a devine gift of God and the peace is also a symbol of God. So get peace, restore peace. By that many kind of powers will awake in body, which are not in a common person. By such kind of concentrated exercise of Aasana the Aasan becomes Siddha means the extreme stage. If some one has gotten Aasan Siddhi, he may achieve a lot of worldly achievements with short works and also may achieve unseen achievements means invisible achievements.

To create a deep concentration it is good and obvious to concentrate inner and outer all powers & organs in that limitless almighty. For it the sky may be taken as a subject inside the brain. By outside eyes if these are open the sky may be seen continuously with half open eyes. Thus the connection with inner and outer world will continue. Laterly the eyes will start to shut by theirselves and concentration will go deep & deep upto the samadhi & God. There are a lot of Aasanas which may be learnt from a good Yoga teacher but Aasanas should never be practiced by the help of book only. Because Aasana create a direct biological change in body and that may be harmful. So various Aasanas have been avoided to describe here.

Results - Tatodwand waa nabhighaatah - Patanjali.

Maharshi Says that by the Siddhi of Aasan the realization of weatheric changes go away the problems & pains of Summer & Winter create no difficulty to Yogi.

D. Praanaayaam :

Pranaayaam said by Maharshi Patanjali is -

Tasmin Sati Shwas Prashwas Yorgativichchhedah Praanaa- yaamah - Patanjali

Now the phase - second which is totally biological & physical starts. By the practices of this part the body is made eligible for Yoga and because the philosphical part is more typical in practice so often this part is started firstly and then other parts are exercised by most of the practitioners.

For Pranayaam Maharshi says after the Siddhi of Aasan this part comes. To know the Siddhi of Aasan it should be analysed that do the summer & winters are not bothering to the practitioner when he sit on an aasan. If it is this stage of no botheration then it should be believed that Aasan is Siddh. After Aasan siddhi the phase comes in which the normal system of breathing is checked and breaked in a particular new way for a short period and that new way of stopping the normal function of in & out breathing is known as Praanaayaam. Thus by this stopping of in & out breathings gives a control on breaths which are the only one measure important factor of life or aliveness.

Bahyabhyantara Stambha Prattiradesh Kaal Sankhyaabhih Paridrishto Deergh Sookshmah - Patanjali.

To explain the praanaayaam Marshi Paatanjali has said that stopping of breaths and controlling of breaths as well as keeping inside and releasing of breaths has three kinds of it. To take in artificially or by own will to keep it inside upto a certain time and then to release it slowly is a new breathing system. By this process the difficulties born or disorders born in natural breathings either naturally born botherations of natural process of breathings go away after some day's practice. the normality of breath as required for body comes in normal process of breathings. In another hand breathing volves, lungs, tubes and several corporate organs of breathing system in and outside of body become normal, fit, healthy and strenghtened. By this way the air goes inside the all over veins and cleans the disturbed walls.Pranayam normalizes all the functions of blood circulations as with normalization of blood circulating organs, veins.

Bahyabhyantara Vishayaxepi Chaturthah - Patanjali.

tubes upto heart. From head to toe several kind of air pressures give a needed and powerful pressure by which all the systems of inner functioning of body go to their normal and natural stages as well they were previously in young days. Excluding this the belly, kidnies, heart digesting system and others also get a real powerful health to activate the inner biological machineries. By this all kind of visible & invisible bodies get a real shape & structures which these should be.

Only by pranayam total system of body becomes fresh cleaned, naturalized, regularized and impowered as per need of the body as per needed balances. The organs, all organs of the body where these are damaged, weak and irregularized they start to their selves restructuring, they start to leave irregularities, they start to be balanced and normal in functions. Many-many kind of diseases of light or heavy nature start to leave the body. By praanaayaam only a body gets a real resistence power against the weather, against the diseases and against the maal meals. The whole digesting system enables and the chemical system of body goes towards the positivity in favour of the body functions.

Tatah Ksheyate Prakaashaa Varanam - Patanjali.

A lot of chemical disturbances take place inside the belly, inside the enzyming machinary, inside the lungs, kidney and heart due to which the normal functions of body become irregularized. But when enough repeatition of praanaayaams as according to the capacity & need of body starts and continues upto long periods all kind of physiologies of an individual take a regularity and it becomes natural.

Thus when chemistry of a body starts to restructure and resettle to itself then the physics & geography of body automatically enables and an individual feels good, gets good results in body. He feels more active, pleased & fit.

Dharnaasu Cha Yogyataa Manasah - Patanjali.

Actually, as already has been said many times that there are five elements in composition of the body. When one element works too much it becomes irregularized and creates many kind of disorders in all over the body. To regularize all such five elements one of them air has been choosen in Praanaayaam. By the help of praanaayaam or by the way of Praanaayaam all other four elements may be regularised upto a certain stage and the rest irregularities may be recovered by water, foods, sleeps awakings and by some other light activities. Whether there is no need of too much details of Praanaayaam because without the help of a real teacher of Yoga no one should practice

Praanaayaam. Because it may become harmful and very harmful upto brain disturbance. So in direction and presence of own teacher praanaayaam is usable.

While praanaayaam also has several kinds of veriety but no more verieties should be adopted only one or two verieties are enough for good health and good results. It needs not to be a person of exibition & fair infact Yoga and Praanaayaam practices are quite personal. As all the Rishis of Yoga has said in ancient periods for circumstances of Yoga that the practices of Yogasana and Praanaayaam must be completed in lonely, peaceful, pious, natural and distrubless places. Because when a person do exercises of Praanaayaam he comes in close contacts of his inner body and inner soul with all invisible inner bodies. And a littlest disturbance of some one's presence, or sound or smell may harm him badly. Thus in place of benefits and fitness a person might be going in harms. So praanaayaam and other excercises never should be completed in crowds, or in presence of others.

There is a big need of natural air but if it is not possible to sit alone upto the practices in a lonely place then it is too better to sit on floor or on hard surface of bed somewhere inside own residence. At least that will not harm by distrubances.

In another hand a little explaination of in, out and keeping Praanaayaam is needed. When a long controlled (desciplined) slow breath is being taken by a practitioner the all body with mind (brain) and heart awakes to take it inside and lungs store air upto their last capacity. When the air is kept till long moments how much a person can bear the machinery of whole body starts fast working upto its last capacity and laterly the capacity increases inside all organs, supply of air reaches upto every vein, tissues and cells. Then after when the air is left slowly with disciplined and controlled rythum all the cells, tissues veins, organs and machinary leave their unwanted mall parts and they supply towards the air existing organs and tubes. By that most of the bad elements go away by the left air.

When the air is kept inside the capacity of lungs and other organs increases. The supplies of air, blood, cosmic energies with enzimes, vitamins fastly goes towards the needed parts and places and within moments it resettles the all organs with the pressures of such kept air inside the lungs. Because the pressure of lungs pressurizes to all veins and veins create a big pressure on all over the body. Another kind of outer Praanaayaam is there in which the air is left out and the empty lungs and middle parts are kept till a few moments in lack of air. By this pranaayaam a big need of air inside the body becomes created and laterly body takes air by it self as per need. By all such kind of pranaayaamas there are two big changes to come in body which have to come - one is the erosioning the covers of lights and to reach upto a real stage. Another one is to get keeping capacity of all powers as well as with the power of keeping concentration as something like, moon, sun, water, fire, air, earth or on God.

E. Pratyaahaar - Keeping :

Maharshi Patanjali says about the pratyahaar.

Swavishyaasamprayogeichittaswaroopaanukaarevendri- yaanaam pratyaahar - Patanjali.

There are five organs known as Indrinya these are the causes of consumption & use of all worldly things in a body these are ear, nose, tongue, skin & eyes.

These all five organs are having a deep relations with five elements every element has it's one organ in body as- sky - has ears, earth has nose, fire has eyes, water has tongue, air has skin.

All five elements also have a lordship on five subjects (vishaya) These are- touch, smell, seen, sound & liquid. These are five subjects. Their attraction, attachment, and the will to use such five subjects are the boundations of a soul. As much one is attached with any one of them or with all. He is tightly bounded with that subject and his organs are slaves of such subjects. Till when a soul is bound in such subjects, till then it can not liberate to it.

For liberation of a soul it's a need too to leave the attachment with all five subjects. And this liberation comes by the practice of leaving their use and by leaving interest as well as attachment of the subject. When a person liberates to him from habits and interests of such subjects he gets his organs and sentiments in no need of such used subjects. Whether this is a very difficult practise but with a strong will and regular practice it is possible. Thus these liberated organs and their all consuming powers go towards the inner section of invisible realizer that is chitta.

When these organs start to live with this inner status of chitta their nature converts as similar to the chitta. When this conversion takes a permanent shape of organs power in shape of chitta that is the complete stage of pratyahar. By this pratyahar the power of organs and the organs come in minimum use of worldly uses. The energy of these organs restores in them and in chitta.

Tatah Paramaa Vashyateindriyaanaam - Patanjali.

Maharshi says that by the complete stage of pratyahar all the organs come in total descipline of the individual and chitta.

When such energy starts to restore in the organs and the usage of organs goes down minimised only for necessities of life. One another stage comes in body and mind. This has too much importance as when the usage of organ reduces in number, in ratio then peace, patience and dovineness enables in a person even all these get an increasement too.

As how much such increasement increases the stages of pure naturality and the stages of devineness also increase. Another a lot of results of Yoga practices which are not complete in results, start to complete their results shortly to bring in body. As the Eashwar Pranidhaan, Praanaayaam, Yamas and Niyamaa also take a strong position in life and in body too. By all such desciplinizations of body organs the arrival of a Yogi inside the devine zone and inside the sector of super natural powers takes a speed. Thus all kind of best possibilities of Yoga results are dependents of the liberation of the organs from their subjects.

If one practitioner has won over four and is getting failure in liberation of only one organ he may fall to the first stage again or he may not reach upto the last stages of Yoga. Though he might be practicing regularily with full devotion on other four organs. To win all five organs its a first one to win the skin and touch the need of sex is a touch. If that one is controlled completely it is easy to control other organs within short periods. After liberating skin one should concentrate on tongue it has two works taste and talk. Boath are big problems in the way of Yoga. Without a total control on organs and on their subjects it is quite impossible to walk the way of next stage of Dhaarnaa means to keep.

F. Dhaarnaa - Concentration :

Maharshi Patanjali says about Dhaarnaa.

Deshbandh Chittasya Dharanaa - Patanjali.

To concentrate the chitta (the inner realizer) on some thing either it is inside the body or it is outside the body, either it is visible or invisible, is Dharanaa. The total power of organs with the power of chitta when concentrates on one target or on one aim that is the stage of Dhaaranaa.

By such concentration many kind of achievements may be gotten which may never be in a non Yogi. Only Yogi can get such results. This practice also should be completed at peacefull places, at least the period of begining stages must need a very peacefull and lonely place where should not be any disturbance at the time of concentration because it also may harm. By disturbances it may create mental disorders. The aims of Dhaaraanaa means such objects on which the chitta may be concentrated and fixed till the late moments. There are a lot of aims, it may be said that each and every thing of visible and invisible world is an object to keep fix the chitta to concentrate.

A few objects for such purpose has been researched and these are. Sun, moon, air, God, water, Deities, elephants, spirit of friendship for all, in the veins circle of belly area of body, inside the neck Valley, at the top part of own hand. By keeping chitta on such objects a lot of knowledges of several kind may come to a person. By such keepings of concentration on sun all knowledge of Bhuvanas comes. (Shortly to know there are fourteen Bhuwanas means, fourteen worlds like Earth - By keeping in elephant, lion or horse the same power comes. Keeping concentration on the hole of top of self head the prophets messangers of God which are quite invisible by normal eyes are seen. By keeping on the circle of of belly all the vein system of body comes in knowledge. By keeping concentration on inside valley of neck the need of hunger & thurst goes out upto the concentration.

By such kind of concentration keeping on different objects, six kind of siddhis (special powers) come in body in other words a person gets a stage, of six kinds of special powers in him. As five organs & one Chitta is controlled & desciplinized in a special descipline of yoga. Every organ gives a very special power as well as with chitta and these all six are.

1. Pratibh - By the discipline of chitta a person may see all things of past present and future. He may see even covered and hidden things too, things which are so away also may be seen. **2. Shraaran** - By ears power the devine words may be heared but not by the years. **3. Vedan** - By the power of skin devine touches may be experienced not only by skin. **4. Aadarsh** - By the power of eyes kept in chitta the devine scenes may be seen. **5. Aaswaad** - By the desciplined power of tongue the devine taste may be tasted. **6. Vaartaa** - By the desciplined power of nose the devine smells may smelled.

G. Dhyaan - Meditation :

Maharshi says - **Tatrapratyayaikataanataa Dhyaanam - Patanjali.**

In Dhyaan and Dhaaranaa there is a little difference of time in keeping concentration on any object. In the stage of Dhaaranaa, the concentration practice is momentary and it is a begining of keeping the concentration. To create a control on concentration. To create a control on concentration - as for a few moments concentration is kept on sun then it is kept on a tree, then after to keep on another object is Dhaarana.

Thus the chitta Gati (the activities and movements) have to keep on orders cf self not on by its own nature. Means the chitta is ever effected and attracted by the worldly means or by usually comming ideas and that is not a stage of control that is its usual nature. By the long practices of Dhaaranaa it starts to live in descipline of the Yogi. When it starts to live in orders then it may be kept every where on any object and that is said Dhyaan means Meditation. In begining the keeping of concentration becomes very momentory but by the practice the concentration goes upto the long periods upto hours, as per need it may be kept and that is a good stage of Meditation.

Although by such kind of Meditation several kind of Siddhi's (Stages of special powers obtained) are obtained which are said in chapter of Dhaaranaa but these are the obstacles & barriers of a Yogi in the way of God. These fore said siddhis are not a result of Dhaaranaa practice In fact all such Siddhis are a result of Meditation/Dhyaan. But these were described in that chapter just to motivate the attention of Yoga practitioners towards the results and objects of Dhaaranaa.

It has been in every kind of Yoga that these siddhis are a big problem of Yogi. So no Yoga practitioner should concentrate on such objects. Because if once a Yogi is slipped in attractions of siddhis he often lives in such siddhis zone only. Due to this barrier a Yogi may not complete his Yoga way. Yogas climax is to join the God to reach upto the God. Whether siddhi zone is a devine sector. But even then these siddhis are only devine conversion of the powers of such organs. Because these siddhis are conversion of energy or power of organs so these are not the real stopages of a Yogi but this 'Siddhi-zone' should be avoided by matured wisdom and strong wills and should go directly to the God.

When a Yogi Meditates on god and ever keeps concentration on God. He gets a real Siddhi of his life. He wins over all five elements permanently for ever. And who wins all such Siddhis of five elements he reaches upto God. When a Yogi reaches to God he becomes lord of such siddhis. He gets a lot of powers of God. He becomes a that drop of water which falls in ocean and becomes ocean. So every Yogi has a big need to keep his object only on God. As the worldly attractions of five elements and their subject attract to a common individual in the same way these siddhis attract to a Yogi.

H. Samaadhi -

The stage of God/Zero : Maharshi Patanjali has said a lot for this as.

Tadevmatranirbhaasam Swaroop Shoonyamiva Samaadhih-Patanjali.

As the developed stages of Dhaarnaa becomes Dhyaan in the same way the developed stages of Dhyaan/Meditation are Samadhi when a person goes in deep and long Meditations in which he forgets his own existence and becomes completely similar to the object that stage is samaadhi. In stage of Samaadhi first of all a stage of Zero comes for a Yogi. Here he forgets all his worldly movements, thoughts, realizations and goes completely in zero.

This Samaadhi has also several kinds and stages here too. The stages of energy conversion in a person continue upto the first steps of Samadhi. Because upto here a lot of seeds of wills, desires and sanskaaraas, memories exist in a shape of minutest shape which are invisible. And if the practices of Yoga has been stopped at this atoms, its not well, as this is needed in this stage. From here, these seeds may again take a shape of complete tree.

Such kind of growings of desires and memories are seen in most of the Yogis. There are rare Yogis who complete their Yoga successfully and reach to God. It is often said by scholars and Rishis that - 'As these are the higher stages of Yoga are there in a life of Yogi the disturbances, obstacles and barriers of such levels are already present there'. So every Yogi should care his self. His practices must be watched and should continue the Yoga practices with deep patience.

With this fact one should continue that as with the mercy of God due to our own practices as we have reached upto this stage in the same way with patience & practice we will reach upto the God. From where we will get complete liberation, full freedom and this worldly boundation will never bother to us.

Trayamekatra Sanyamah - Patanjali.

The stage of being on one object at one time equally with Dhaaranaa Dhyaan and samaadhi is said sanyam. After winning this stage means when a yogi successfully goes upwards from this stage too then the lights of wisdom and knowledge come to a person as a siddhi of this stage. This kind of several stages of siddhis come in the way of Yoga. But ever should live like a new practitioner. Again one should start to again concentrate one by one- on earth, water, fire, air & on sky. By this the winning of all five elements and sanskars as well as with memories repeat their selves. By this repeatition the seeds of all kind of desires again goes removed. By this a new era of Samaadhi comes to a Yogi and that is known as Nirbeej Samadhi.

There are two kinds of Samadhi Sabeej (with seeds) and Nirbeej (without seeds). In begining every one starts with seeds. Because the seeds of desires and behavior exist inside minutely. After a few days of regular practices the possibilities of Nirbeej Samadhi come. As well the minutest existence of inside desires and practices of worldly world are washed by practices the stages of the Nirbeej Samadhi come.

Many times in Yoga practices the desires and minute practices of world are not washed but these are just pressed down under the practices and when the times come such seeds grow up again. This Samadhi is known as **Sabeej Samadhi**. This stage needs to practice again upto the complete cleanness.

There is a stage of mind inside the body by which it thinks continuously on worldly subjects whether body is not consuming these all. This habit and nature of mind must be changed upto think on God only. No other subject should be inside the mind. By this the deep and real concentrated stage comes in one that is the result of samadhi.

Tajjayatepragyaalokah - Patanjali.

There are two kind of nature of inner self. In them one is to go to motion less ness or Wave less ness and another is wave ness. By practice boath inner natures go in one stage of motion less ness it comes in boath. No waves come then and that is Nirbeej Samaddhi.

By Samadhi a lot of powers come in one's life these are - **(a)** Ability to know all three times - Past, Present & Future **(b)** To know the dialects of other lives **(c)** To know about the past births of self and of others **(d)** The ability of reading of other's mind by the concentration.

By concentrating on self body and on its structure the Yogi may become invisible for others. Because his relationship with other's eye rays breaks, then the persons may not see him.

Trayamantarang Poorvebhyah - Patanjali.

By concentrating on Karma (deeds) the knowledge of death comes. There are two kind of Karma - Soepkram (deeds paying results in present) Nirupkram (deeds which are not resulting in present there will result in future).

Tadapi Bahirangam Nirbeejasya - Patanjali.

When a Yogi starts to (see) concentrate the serial of results of one's deeds that which one is resulting in present and when it will complete, then what is going to come. By that he goes upto the knowledge of death.

One stage comes for a Yogi where the covers of lights of knowledge or wisdom ends and no kind of imagination and thoughts exist there in a Yogi. That stage of quite emptyness of all worldly & devine phase too creates a stage of samadhi known as Mahavidehaa. This means without body, he really forgets his body and its feelings & realizations.

When a Yogi concentrates his self on the elements' materialistic shape, its minute stage, and on its Analysis or on its Atoms and it means on its existence stages in all circumstances.

Vyathannirodha Sanskaryaoh Abhibhavaproddurbhavan Nirodhkshan Chittanyayo Nirodh Parinamah - Patanjali.

It means shapes of every element materialistic shape, minute shape, its atomic stage and lastly the total existence stages. By such concentrating practice on all such five elements the Yogi gets again very special siddhis.

These siddhis are again more powerful than the previous siddhis and these are **(a) Anima -** to go as minute with all body as an Atom. **(b) Laghima** to loose the total weight of body like air **(c) Mahima** to make so big to his body as a mount or more than that from earth to sky **(d) Garima** to create weight in body or to make body so heavy in weights un imaginably **(e) Prapti** to get any worldly and devine thing within moments **(f) Praakaamya -** will of worldly things to be fulfilled without no barrier **(g) Vashitva** to get descipline and order on all five elements and on those all materials and things which are created by these all five elements **(h) Eashitva** to create all such creations of five elements either these were in past or these are presently some where in world and to rule on all such five elements creation.

Tasya Prashant Vaahitaa Sanskaaraat - Patanjali.

After these siddhis a stage of another kind of siddhis come and these are:-

Kaaya Sampat : The body becomes hard like iron, power comes and beauty of body & face comes.

Indriyajay : Then the again victory comes on organs & chitta. Then after three other kind of Siddhis come and these are - Speed as fast as mana (thoughts) to realize the all five subjects without body - Vikram, then Pradhaanjay means ruling power on nature

Kramaanyatram Parinavnanyatvei Hetuh - Patanjali.

The next stage of Samaadhi comes in which the Yogi lives only with two realizations the individual & the wisdom. In this stage he gets a lord ship on all realizations & sarvagyataa - (the knowingness of all).

Tatah Punah Shamtoditan Tulya Pratyayan chittasyaikagrataa Parinanah - Patanjali.

And when Yogi comes in stage of disattachment of all these then he gets the Kaivalya

Samadhi. After this stage too their are three stages to win to a Yogi after this victory the Yogi gets the real kaivalya Samadhi in which he lives in stage of God. In this stage the realization of wisdom & individual also becomes pious & pure. To reach upto the stage of samadhi there are several otherways. As a few exercises are there which have been previously said in the chapter of Ashtang Yoga are also the way & causes to reach upto the stage of samadhi.

The other methods & ways of Samaadhi are these -

Nirodh - To stop the all movements & waves of chitta is the way of kaivalya by leaving all things and by practicing the Yoga desciplines the stage of stopping comes.

Eshwar Pranidhan - Another way is Eashwarpranidhaan means devotion, dependency and dedication on God. So trust on God firstly. He is the only power of powers, cause of all causes, way of all ways and solution of all problems even he is the solution of solutions.

Mantra - By repeatition of Mantra all kind of difficulties go away from the way of Yogi and he achieves the Samaadhi stage. Kaivalyam.

Praanaayaam - till a long period doing regular practice of pranaayaam continuously Yogi also reaches upto the Kaivalyam.

Concentration & Meditation - By concentrating on any object which is choosen and liked object. It also creates a control from minute atoms to that universe and stage of samadhi comes.

There are many kind of Samaadhis as according to the different stages like- Savitark Samadhi, Nirvitark Samadhi, Sabeej Samaadhi, Nirbeej Samaadhi etc. All such Samaad his also give a stage of Kaivalya, after some time. ❑

PEARL

EFFECTS OF YOGA

Yoga or any kind of action creates reactions in universe, littlest one action effects the universe certainly.

Yoga effects a person in this way that his normal functions of life, body and psychology get a little stop for a short period thoughts, sentiments and biological fun-ctier ing of body get a rest for a short period thus peace, patience, pleasure start to stay, enable & increase in body. If these are no more than all these needed powers and energies of body start to regenerate. Chemical functions of body start to become natural as these were in very young age days. Thus the age effect of body decreases shortly and after a long period of practice it becomes well, without any medicine or liquor.

Dependency of medicines and drugs goes out of the body. Physical fitness and the natural functions of body come in body so fastly. If practitioners is a very young age chap of 10 to 15 years he gets highly improved his mental, psychological and physical energies and peace, patience, wisdom, stemna and pleasure.

A lot of negative minerals, enzymes, gasses and others become stored in body which bother to an individuals body from natural functions of body and that's why a person looses his own natural nature. He adopts unknowingly a different unwanted nature and behaviour due to that he ever feels uneasy uncomfort in his slept or subconscious mind. But when he comes in the way of yoga he starts to regret his natural stages of body and natural nature of his personality as well as with the improved several potencies and steminas for which he deserves.

A lot of tensions of mind, a lot of stresses of his body automatically go away. The comfortable, easy, normal natural stages of mind and body start to came. Due to these changes an individual again gets his body, heart, brain, wills, sentiments well young and powerful. This is the secret of yoga functions in human body. Deep sleeps normal, attitudes, pleasant head, pleased mood and several other positive behaviours and natures of body and personality improve within weeks.

A lot of courage, encouragements, good feelings and divine realizations starts. By that an individuals life pleases and works successfully in all fields of life. That needs only a little investment of time for yoga practices. Whether the life principle practices need no time separately. Wherever you are you can continue the practice- like, truth, non-violence, cleanliness, piousness, no thefting etc.

In fact in modern life there was a lot of problems for which an individual goes in mental tensions. These tensions create several kind of stresses in their veins of body. This vein stress often becomes permanent in that body which one is working all the year. These stresses make abnormal to the biological body and to normal natural psychological, elemental and ideological personality.

Thus when someone goes through studies of yoga and yoga's nature he gots comfort and real hopes in his mind. So the deep studies of yoga philosophy are must. Because when an individual starts study deeply he feels that what he has lost and how easily he can regain his own powers, eligibilities again even other several powers too, by simple practices this is magic of yoga.

When an individual's so long and old stresses looses and natural stage of body starts to come, a lot of physical problems, mental, psychological and personality problems go out, many diseases go out by the urine and latrine. Magically a person feels normal, natural, fit and pleased. Depressions, anxieties and tiredness goes away. A new era of body and life starts. He gets that life is not so difficult he may live pleasantly and may get a lot.

When stresses starts to go in stage of relax and natural stage brain earns the lost peace and power, heart works better, new thoughts doesn't seem burden but they encourage for life and life starts again. Only these fitnesses are not results and effects of yoga religious, spiritual and super natural world's door also seem opened for such yoga practitioner. ❑

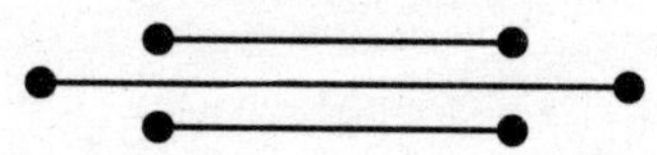

PEARL

EXPERIMENTS OF YOGA

Yoga is theoretical and practical booth. All kinds of yogas have their own philosophies, experiments and exercises. Here in this book the Ashtaang yoga said by Mahrshi Patanjali is the subject basically.

People believe or not believe is not a subject in yoga, but the subject is this that do people do the exercises of yoga regularly. If one is doing continuously only one exercise of yoga just to examine the truth of yoga. It is sure that after a certain period of his continuous practice in life the exercise will start to result in his life.

Whether a lot of exercises of yoga has already been discussed shortly in a chapter previously but even then a few exercises to examine the reality of yoga is being discussed. **(a)** Truth, **(b)** Non Violence **(c)** Disattachment, **(d)** Pranayam, **(e)** Aasan, **(f)** Others.

Just by these practices yoga may be examined and a lot of human virtuous and hidden powers of a person will become enabled.

A. Truth :

What is truth ? **(i)** What something is happening to say, to convey and to write as it is, is truth. **(ii)** God only is the real truth. **(iii)** What an individuals life is 'to live and to show it, as it is' is a truth **(iv)** Wordly truth is the nearest one fact to the God and by following truth in all over life speaking and living no one can speak a lie infront of that person. Even the realizations of God and Supenatural powers will start.

B. Non-violence :

This all creation is created by God and if someone harms to all these creatons God never pleases with him.So never kill, never pain to others nor to human neither to other lives. Even to plants trees, and to natural things. Do not ruin, do not harm. Within year you will get very positive results of this practice.The prophets of God, the messangers of God will stasrt to heop you, to guide you. The realizations of God will start to you.

As because of this fact that every creation is a creation of God like me. I must love them and to these all.Start a friendship with all creatoins you will get that all other lives including the God will help you they will lick you.And many times they will talk to you. And when all such creations will start to realize and feel you their real friend by heart God will feel you his believed child. Honestly just think for welfare of such lives. The day will come when you will be understanding their languages and body languages too. Its not unbelievable within one year you will become a friend of them and within three year syou will undestand their conversations. Their new words you will start to understand clearly and lateraly by their help you may understand their languages. It has not a big need of works just leave eating fresh eggs you will see they like you not only this but by their well wishes you will get several successes in life.

C. Disattachment:

All wordly meetings as in shape of any relations are very new in this birth you have gotten. But due to deep attachemnts with people and world you are in deep pains leave all these attachments. Believe in this fact that as much you will release the sentiments and feelings of attachment you will liberate yourself from several sentimental pains and grips. You will feel yourself free more and more daily by daily. Yes attach yourself with God, with that almighty you will be enabled, fresh and pleased day will come you will need no one.

D. Pranayam:

Chemistry, biology and psychology are also dependents of elements - when deep problems are there in one's mind naturally he becoems concentrated in these and flow of energy goes towards that. After a long period someone may become disordered. But by exercises of Pranayam an individuals such problem comes tonatural stage within moments and by continuation it continues to live natural.

E. Aasan:

A lot of difficulties andproblems with several diseases and abnormalities come in body after passing the years in life struggles. Veins leave the proper supplies of blood, enzymes' production rate falls, air supplies inside the body become abnormal and chemistry of body becomes poor due to that biology, geography and also leave their nature in very young ages of 40 and 50 persons feel sick. To leave all these problems back, start yoga's Aasanas practices adopt only 5 for beginning within week get results. Yoga is not a magic but it gives the results like magic.

F. Others:

Many many other exercises of Yoga are their which may give you a power, stemna which is so fresh, natural and surprising. Like, if you concentrate yourself on air even you will reduce your body weight and if you concetnrate on earth you will start getting weight. Yes there are several ways. ❑

BENEFITS OF YOGA

(a) Regaining self powers, (b) Achievement of new powers, (c) Living well, (d) Financial Benefits, (e) Achievements of sucesses, (f) Enabling the soil, (g) Pleasing the God.

Whether benefits of yoga are unacountable but a few kind of general benefits are being described here so that persons may understand that what they expect from the world and by their lives that all may be achieved by the way of Yoga. It may be said that since the history of Yoga had been started billions of people had been benefitted and still today millions of people are in process. They are getting benefits of yoga. Children, young, men and women all may get such.

A. Regaining Self Powers :

Memory, thinking power, digestion power, smile, resistance power, deep sleeps, power of taste of tongue, hearing power of years, seeing power of eyes, benting power of backbone, flexibility of body, patience, peace, pleasure, courage, hopes, will power, ambitions and several other kind of steminas with resistance powers, everybody is loosing fastly in todays world. But no one want to loose it every one want to get it again and Yoga gives it back.

B. Achievement of New Powers :

As the loosen powers of an individual may be regained in the same way the new powers may be achieved as more hunger, more thrust, more digestion, more deep sleeps, more freshness, several kind of wisdoms, many kind of impressing power, working powers, collapse of cowardish, courage, bravery, devotion, pity, leniency, politeness, supernatural rights, sight by which a person can see in all over world from one place, even upto the other place. Except this several other kind of powers including wordly powers like political success, success in literature and in finance too, whether this is not coming in a day but comes.

C. Living Well :

If an individual can get back his powers and peace he also can get a few new powers. He starts to live well as previously he was living at the days of his well and healthy body. When a person comes in yoga way he starts to know the realities and facts of life. Then a new era of life starts to live and in that he lives well than his previous days. It is also the real benefit of Yoga.

D. Achievements of Successes :

When a person regains lost physical powers and when he achieves new powers he starts to use his self in a very calculative way and he achieves many successes.

As one person gets a little new success his confidence enables and he gets a new life around him, he starts to walk a way of successes.

When a person has good physical, mental and psychological powers naturally he becomes more deserving than others and gets success upto his life.

E. Financial Benefits :

Till when a person is living completely this wordly world he needs a lot of expenses but when he starts Yoga automatically several expenses which are not necessary go away and he starts to live in minimum means. By that he saves and by increasing his power he works better and earns better.

F. Enabling the Soul :

Due to the wordly involvements the divine virtuous of the soul become so weak due to that soul also become weak. But a person who starts Yoga practices the washing of his soul starts. The wordly thing's extra burden come down and the divine virtuous start to come again. By that the freshness, pleasure, peace and pious love for all comes in a person. When a soul liberates itself from wordly surroundings it becomes pure.

G. Pleasing the God :

Yes there is God and there are several ways to reach the God. Yoga is the easy and best way to please the God and to reach the God. By Yoga a lot of dirty things of heart and thoughts goes out gradually and a person becomes pious and pleasant. God loves to them who are trying to disciplinize their lives in religious or spiritual disciplines. Excluding this the body itself has several stoppages in it which are doors of different stages and in these one door also opens in the Kingdom of God. ❑

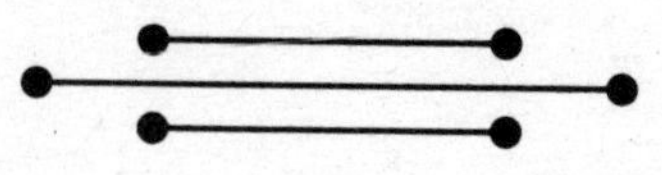

PEARL

POWERS OF YOGA

A lot of powers of yoga are there, these may not be counted. Yoga reaches upto the God, but for a normal yoga practitioner general powers are being discussed here. These are also too much but a few of them are these :

(a) Power of naturalization of body, (b) Power of disease protection, (c) Power of Elemental energy growing, (d) Power of human virtuous enabling, (e) Power of stamna enabling, (f) Power of resistance developing, (g) Power of super natural powers sector joining

A. Power of Naturalization of Body :

In life struggles, and in today's life styles naturally the naturality of body goes down. Due to many kind of weaknesses an individual may feel that people are suffering due to such unnaturalities of body. Medicines, dietings, naturapathies and others can not care as well the Yoga makes body natural. When a chemically disordered body comes in Yoga practices all kind of bodies start to be fit and shortly a person becomes fit.

B. Power of Disease Protection :

Due to many unwanted eatings and drinks, human body's several things go in disorder biologically. These mall eatings might be restored inside the body upto a long period and sickness may became a nature of body. But when a such body starts very light exercises of yoga the nature of body again moves towards its natural stage and diseases go away.

C. Power of Elemental Energy growing :

Yoga is the way by which an individual may normalize and create a balance of elemental energies. Not only this but after normalizing its stages the restoring capacity of elemental energies may be increased. And when the restoring capacity of such energies comes in body, its growth also increases. By that growth and restoring capacity the body may be kept alive till the long period as well as upto its life.

D. Power of Human Virtuous Enabling :

When a common individual comes in field of yoga he has very least power of human virtuous on his body. But when he starts Yoga his slept human virtuous and their powers awake in body. These take a real shape and growth by which an individual achieves worldly successes and lives pleasant. These human virtuous help a person in developing social, political, financial and friendly relations and become ladders of success.

E. Power of Resistance Developing :

Resistance power is a big power of body. To resist the diseases, to resist the heat, to resist the cold, to resist the pains, to resist the winds on and by a body is very necessary and natural need of a person. This is the power of human body which keeps body well and healthy till the long period. Several wrong items which are harmful for body are sometimes taken. If a body has enough resistance power such items', harms go minimum to a body working capacity also enables.

F. Power of Stemna Enabling :

All of kind of stemnas of body are the real physical powers like to walk till the miles, to work till the hours, to eat well and enough, to bear enough cold and heat. To keep patience till the long periods even in pains. Stemna to bear loads and to live in minimum means. To talk till the hours, to please a lot of persons. To face the adverse environments. Stemna to live in plain, mounts and on coastal geographical regions too. All these may be developed by yoga practices.

G. Power of Super Natural Powers' Sector Joining :

As it has been said already that Supernatural powers exist there. These are having many varieties in them good or bad, helping or disturbing, lenient and cruel. As an individual has practiced good human virtuous then the good supernatural powers meet and if the nature of practices of exercises was not pious religious approaching the negative powers may join the human body of practitioner and that may become a big problem. Yoga has a power to carry a person upto these supernatural powers zone. After regular reachings upto this zone many or at least one super natural power comes in contact of exerciser. In Beginning the exerciser joins to this zone and to these powers which are having thousand times better power than humans. Laterally they take such bodies as their colony and they keep relations till long periods. By their helps a person can reach upto sky in success. ❑

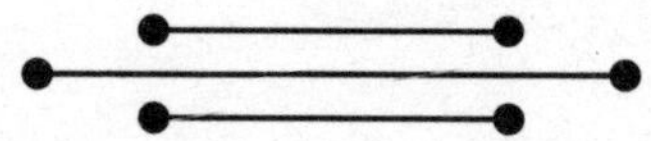

SUPER NATURAL POWERS OF YOGA

As inside the wordly world a world is running in the same way an unseen world is also working in the universe which is the real controller and demonstrator of this seen world. The unseen world has been also designed by that almighty God to look after this seen world. That unseen world has a lot of varieties of super natural powers inside it. A few are deities, a few are souls, a few are kinds of deities and a few are sub-deities.

In them a few are controllers of wealth, a few are controllers of wisdom and knowledge, a few are lords of power, a few are lords of natural things and a few are lords of all bodies. Thus when a person goes in the way of Yoga, after a certain stages of Yoga, he joins that unseen world and these deities help to such yoga person. They give directions and powers to such persons.

In other hand such super powers nominate such individuals as their representatives in this world. They use such persons to fulfill several very special projects in the world. But not all the times. Even then such super powers ever help to their contact persons, and a common individual becomes very special than his past times. A common person becomes spiritual.

These super natural powers are just a variety of God powers. By these powers the Almighty God creates many many new faces and designs of the world, by which he needs to fulfill his targets, Excluding these the super powers are too much powerful than the normal individuals. They may change the happenings and faits of the persons. They may relieve all kind of difficulties of a person within moments, or they may create various kind of difficulties for an individual.

These super natural powers may create a lot of chances of life for an individual even they can change the short time death chances too. Such super natural powers have paid a lot of kinds of means to several persons. Excluding this such super natural powers may give any kind of extra powers of any field by which a person may become very special too much powerful, excellent, genius, rich or several other benefits of such kind may become by them to a person of yoga.

Because these super natural powers are lords of various natural things, elements and powers like - Varuna is lord of waters, Agni is lord of lights, fires and heats, Vaayu is lord of winds, airs and storms., There are forty nine Marudganas which are parts of Vayu. In the same way earth is lord of smell and all wealth, Aakash is lord of words, sounds and space.

Excluding these five elemental super natural powers or deities with many many sub deities of these five are there. There are a lot of departments of God which are looked, governed and served by such super natural powers. A few kinds of super natural powers with name are being discussed for the learners of Yoga.

Pretas, Pisaachas, Brahmraxasas, Pitras, Gandharvas, Kinnars, Yaxas, Koosmandas, Bhairavas and Yoginis are there which have complete races of their inside unseen world. Except these many others are existing inside this universe. Who come in contact of a yoga practitioner as the yoga practitioner achieves eligibility.

As one yoga exerciser has crossed a natural range of human powers. It means if a yoga practitioner is doing well and he reaches to the best limits of human powers and reaches to the boundaries of pretas certainly a preta of yoga field starts to guide and help to such person.

Then after as he reaches to Pitar stage one pitar starts to help him and from another boundary of yoga another unseen super power starts to help and practitioner reaches to the deities. Then to God and then to total liberation of soul. Which is the goal of life.

These super natural powers are very helpful to persons if some one gets good relations with them. They try to help in wordly life too. They create a chance to earn good and enough money. They create virtues in a person, they try to make well someone's life.

Even they help to fulfill the ambitions of life if these are good, pious and if these are not harming to others. In other hand the physical and mental powers also enable magically ❑

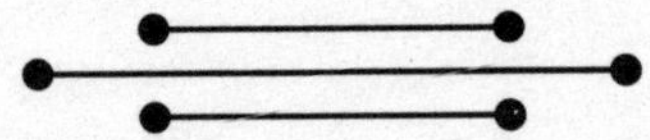

PEARL

ELIGIBLE INDIVIDUALS OF YOGA

From a young chap of 12 years to any age old person is an eligible person of yoga. But very old persons whose body has became totally unfit may not do yoga. Girls, boys, men, women of any age may do exercises of yoga. But for yoga exercises it's a need of a few prerequisites and these are little change of personal life style. First of all smoking is must to leave, then liquors, drugs and all kind of non vegetarian foods should have to leave for ever. And one should study yoga books so deeply till one month at least so that he may know the basics of yoga and may be aware of yoga philosophy and to its principles. In another hand awaking and sleepings also must be changed. It needs early to bed and early to rise. No too much eatings may be allowed. One time in a day take full belly meals as per need of hunger and one meal should be light then after light breakfast twice in a day. First average food must be taken in morning upto 8 or 9 a.m. Tea coffee should be avoided or at least its repetition of many times must be avoided.

Unnecessary talks, unnecessary works, sleeping in late nights must be avoided because all these are very harmful. Its a thing to know for every one that a person do several kinds of activities in a day and in all over the life. In them many activities are very harmful for body and life. Like sleeping in late nights and after the sunrise is a cause of weakness of nervous system. The tissues and cells loose their tightness and youngness by that their functions go slow. Due to weak nervous system many of the biological problems and brain problems start. Thus by changing the daily life style and the meals a person changes his many things by that the naturality comes, which is the base and target of life and yoga too. Persons who have a deep patience and may live continue in new life management as well as with the exercises of yoga. Persons who believes on the words of ancestors, Rishis and yoga teacher too, they are eligible persons of yoga.

Who are really interested to change their life, who are wishing to improve their lives are eligible persons. Who may keep control on their habits and on their several wills are the eligible persons. Who may keep Brahmcharya till long periods are the eligible persons of Yoga Because without Brahmcharya no yoga exercises may give good results.

Who do not have faith on God he may also be a good exerciser of yoga but who may not change his life styles, who may not keep control on his tongue and on sex, he may not be a good and eligible person of yoga.

Who reads well and tries to understand the yoga philosophy deeply he may be the good curious person of yoga. Without deep curiosities and without deep interest no one can learn yoga properly. Deep studies of yoga are a need. But to take only one book by Maharshi Patanjali is the base and that must be learnt by an individual who is coming to this field.

After reading several books by the help of yoga teacher a book must be selected as a base book for ever. Because the help and dependency on many books may be confusing. So its also a need of yoga trainee that he must trust on his teacher. Thus only devotion and trust on Master with a polite behaviour is the eligibility of yoga entrance. ❑

PEARL

YOGA EXERCISE AND LIFE MANAGEMENT

For yoga exercises only half an hour is sufficient. Actually Yoga has two parts for exercises, one is the part of life principles and another is physical exercises. The measure part of yoga is life principles' part by which someone's psychology and ideology becomes neat, clean and pious. By this part an individual goes in changes of life style. Actually it is the basic theme of yoga by which first of all a person learns the meanings of life.

The exercises of life principle part doesn't need extra time. Only a few changes in personal behaviour are needed. These are the attitudes of life which are the need and base of human life. Purity of views and faith on God starts to come in life then the powers of such principles come in an individual. It needs no extra time - as to speak truth and to speak only needed words is a little change of behaviour. When a person will speak truth and will speak minimum words he will restore his energy which will enable his truthful life. In the same way non violence will make a person total vegetarian by which a lot of biological, psychological problems will become solved. Millions of cattles, birds, fishes which are afraid of him will leave fear from his side. They will feel friend to him and too much money will be not wasted in non-vegetarian meals which are so costly than vegetarian meals. Thus a burden of finance will also slightly go down.

For physical exercise part as - Aasan, Pranayam, Dhyaan etc. half an hour is enough in morning. If someone starts yoga the life process changes slightly as he will need to leave the bed in early morning for Yoga exercise of physical part. The early morning is the best time in all over the day. As because of this fact that before the sunrise, awakings and to practice exercises of yoga store much more natural energy in body. All five elements enable with this process. Health becomes fit. And brain tissues get energy for all the day these simple changes in life style change the life attitude and the behaviour also gets changes.

Alcohol, drugs, cigarette and unnatural eatings automatically leave the persons. They get a lot of courage and will power by Yoga to leave the all mal eatings and behaviours. Life becomes strong for life.

Today's ultra modern life is creating biggest problems for life and yoga changes all such non adoptable lifestyle. If someone is ready to make his life good then he needs to remanage his life and for that Yoga is the best way.

All kind of abnormalities in life go away. It may be said that from leaving bed to going the bed life needs amendments and a new management. Yoga designs new life managements even waters, eating, drinking, talking, works, sleeping, behaviour, thoughts phychology, ideology all are the parts of yoga. Today persons do, persons live but unfortunately several things has been forgotten from life styles. And these things and styles were only for welfare of individuals.

A new life management starts, anew life philosophy comes, a new world of life comes and people feel very energetic, fresh, pious, divine and hopeful.

Really if a person devotedly comes in way of Yoga he gets his life changed magically. That all is a real life management. To live with minimum means and with minimum expenses is a gift of yoga. So this is the best one way of life. ❑

PEARL

YOGA & PRACTICAL LIFE

Today's life is the fastest one life of the human race. Every one is suffering from problems and tensions. Everyone is facing irritations. Everyone is trying to achieve more and more achievements within short period. Life struggles are giving a lot of stresses. So individuals are loosing their biological and mental powers in short periods. Excluding this social and family tensions are not so lesser. Even personal lives of every one are passing through very stresses.

Thus the life has became like a war field and everyone is bothered every one needs success, peace and pleasure. But crowds and lack of means in world as in ratio of population are the cause of imbalance of luxuries for each one. So how an individual may live peacefully. Because the peace is not obtained by the means only it is a thing of inner world and this peace and patience is being loosed by most of the persons in life struggles. So when they get success they get theirselves empty by their physical and mental powers. Their enjoying stemna of the luxuries losses in a way of achievements.

But yoga helps in all these problems when an individual is struggling for life he may save much energy of his body than normal livings and he may perform better results by the help of yoga. He may keep peace, patience and pleasure in his body at the time of struggles. Not only this but also he may recollect his own lost energy and powers by the way of yoga. Some one can improve his working capacity and may sleep well as with the help of yoga exercises

Thus the practical life of any one may be improved better upto best by the help of yoga. Even the spiritual, religious and supernatural powers also may be improved, achieved within the way of practical life. Only a little use of time of daily life is sufficient for yogic exercises.

In fact yoga is not only for those people who are only spiritual or religious but yoga is for all kinds of persons, who have to work hard and who need to work much more mental works Either who do not need any work all kind of people may be benefitted by Yoga exercises. It improves the life ❑

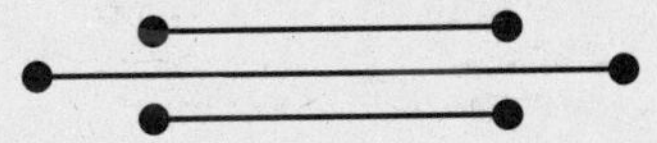

PEARL

RELEVANCY OF YOGA IN MODERN LIFE

Really the inventions of all kind of yoga are so old and very ancient but this is the magic that this is ever modern for all lives and for human life. Today or after many centuries, the way of yoga will help to the human life in living their life. Actually, a few persons think that Yoga is very typical and ancient. Yes they think right. It is typical and ancient but till when someone is not entering in the field of yoga he is afraid of its typicality and oldness. But when someone starts it to know and comes in the way of its simple and little exercises he feels that yoga is the most relevant way of life. And this kind of people often say that yoga is the only way which is ever relevant in any period and age for human life. Because when a modern person is passing through the problems of anxiety, stresses, half sleeps or sleeplessness and hopelessness the yoga creates a new life in the body and the failure feelings convert in energy of success and positiveness. So the yoga is ever relevant for all.

When a mountain of problems is infront of an individual and so deep trenches of life are around him, its natural to be hopeless. But yoga encourages in those moments, yoga gives patience and energy for all that and yoga enables for the life struggles even it pays peace and pleasures in the works. Actually this is the era of yoga in all over the world. Its a record growth period of yoga practitioners in world. Everyone is suffering from the problems and everyone is facing the stresses. Where is the way by which problems may be faced? That is the way of yoga by which the loosing courages, loosing patience, loosing stemna and potency, loosing pleasure may be kept safe. A lot of number of people is in all over the world who have gotten a new smile for their same life by the way of yoga and they have won over their problems by their own efforts, and that because became possible for them by yoga. In other many ways of life persons may deceive in your results. But in the way of yoga there is no chance of deceiving because when once you start yoga practices all kind of achievements and results are being and coming in your own body and from that no one can take only you can use all that. ❑

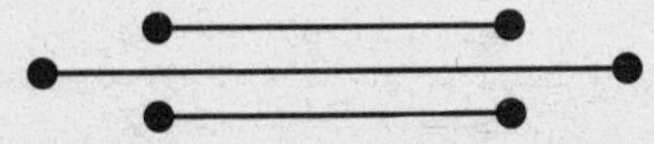

PEARL

YOGA MASTERS & TRAINEES

Whenever an individual needs to go by the way of yoga first of all he must know kinds of yoga and then the selection of one kind should be made final with deep and real thinking. As prem yoga, bhakti yoga are the different fields of yoga and karmayoga, kriyayoga are different fields. Then after Sankhya and Sanyaas yoga are also different fields of yoga. But by all kind of yoga an individual may get good results of life for selecting yoga one should go through all kind of such books.

As a first master of yoga good books are best. The original text books are the best guide like - for all kinds of basic knowledge one should go through Srimad Bhagwadgeeta, then for Sankhyayoga Patanjali Yoga Darshan should be choosen. For Bhaktiyoga a lot of books are there in Indian Religious Literature. At least 3 to 5 times the basic book of the choosen yoga must be studied thoroughly for Sankhya Yoga also read Geeta. For Ashtang Yoga Patanjali Yog Darshan should be studied. And basic practices of life principles should start by self. After being practiced well of yam-niyam one should go to a good master of yoga who must be a deep scholar of yoga philosophy then after the later practices should be started in guidance of Master.

In fact due to speedy promotion of yoga and acceptance by people the false masters have been born in several markets, even from India to abroad. So, must choose a good scholar of yoga philosophy. Because Yoga is a life philosophy it has much philosophical and ideological part than yogasanas.

Master must be master and tranee must be a good pupil. A very Good learner, polite person, disciplined, believing and may learn and practice well. Such kind of learner may do good and best results within short period. There are two ways to learn and know it properly, either follow without much more questions and get results or do all questions be satisfied of your problems and then start. But continue study of best books of yoga everyday when you are practicing. ❑

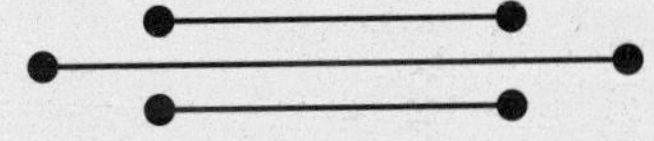

PEARL

THE CLOSING

An individual puzzled and bothered by the personal and worldly problems. A person depressed and lost hopes, tries to recollect and regather him to live his life. A person struggling with life and circumstances for life and life means, doesn't know that who and what he is. How much potency, capability and powers he has inside him. A person of such stages doesn't know that still he has a power to win over the whole nature not only a few worldly means.

Its an obvious stage of a person who never had heard about such human powers, how he can think or imagine for all that? What he is seeing? What he is hearing and what he is facing that becomes his life, his real life with several pains and problems, he passes the days of his life. In very difficult struggles from where he never gets enough as according to his needs and expectations. Thus life goes wasted in a simple way.

A man should know that for a human life there is a big need of a life philosophy to live. Without any life philosophy what a person will live? In India since the ages people are doing researches on life and on the supplements and solutions of life.

As for understanding the fact as life factors India worked on every field, factor and facts - like dress, food, behaviour, thoughts, deeds, works, livings, religion, spirit and on earth and every kind of sciences. Today's world's most prominent, Science developments and other developments are nothing in comparison of Indian researches and works.

These Indian scholars were went to sky, went to waters, went to fires, went to each and every thing visible and invisible. Who can compare this knowledge with these researches?

Even they worked on the thoughts and sentiments of life. They described several disciplines of life in shape of life philosophies. Yoga is one of them, which is never old, it is ever young, which ever keeps young to its practitioners, so go with Yoga philosophy and with Yoga by that you will get life. ❑

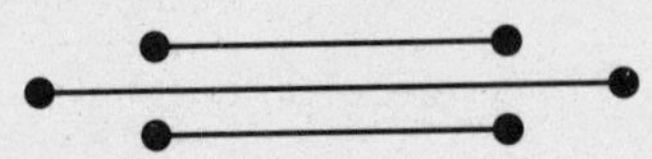